# LEEDS
# MEMORIES

*The publishers would like to thank the following companies for their*

*support in the production of this book*

## Main Sponsor
## Andrew Page Limited

Bellow Machine Company
Bray Burners
Brethericks
Brooke North, Solicitors
W Button and Company Limited
City Varieties Music Hall
DePuy International Limited
Dodgson Funeral Service
Grand Theatre & Opera House
Jones of Oakwood
Jowett and Sowry Limited
J & L Marshall Building Supplies
LHF Healthplan
George E Lowe Limited
Lynn & Jones
McCarthy's of Leeds
Northern Ballet
Opera North
Redmayne-Bentley Stockbrokers
The Last Viceroy
Turner & Townsend Group
WABCO Automotive UK Limited
Wallace Arnold
West Yorkshire Playhouse
Yorkshire Television

First published in Great Britain by True North Books Limited
England HX3 6AE
01422 344944

ISBN 1 903204 62 3

*Text, design and origination by True North Books Limited*
*Printed and bound by The Amadeus Press Limited*

# LEEDS
# MEMORIES

# *Contents*

# Introduction

Whenever we meet anyone for the first time and we enter into the ritual of introducing ourselves, having got rid of the step of exchanging our names, there comes the inevitable question, 'Where do you come from?' Assumptions are made about our personalities, as if our place of birth influences our growth. We believe it ourselves, so why shouldn't others that we meet? 'I went to that school', we say with pride. 'It was a good school', we add, thus making it clear that we are well educated. 'We lived in that street', we say, usually turning glassy-eyed as we remember those wonderful days. 'We were poor but happy', we add, knowing that such a heritage added steel to our character. Suddenly time filters out all the bad things, and our life's hard knocks are forgotten and we remember mainly sunshine. For those who make fun of us, we have a book like this one, which we can place before them and say; 'Do you remember...?', and very soon they too are strolling down Memory Lane.

The more we investigate the past and the more we seem to have in common. How many times in our lives do we say to people, 'If we talk any longer we will be related.'?

Celebrating Victory in Europe in May 1945.

So exactly what are our roots, and where do we begin to be influenced by them? This question interests many today as they search for their family tree in the town libraries and archives. It is important to know our roots for they contain the ingredients of our character and personality. If we gaze at the pages to follow with someone a little older than ourselves by our side, we will find that they add a little more depth to our recollections of Leeds. We soon realise that we receive some of our attitudes from the stories that our parents and grandparents told us. They will remember the days before the Inner Ring Road ploughed a furrow through the centre. With the aid of this book, and the nostalgic pictures it contains, they mentally walk the streets of the city, before they were pedestrianised. Hopefully the captions, which accompany the photographs, will bring the surprised gasp, 'Well, I never knew that!'.

We have only to travel a short distance from the centre of this busy city to discover beautiful countryside, and historic buildings. There is much evidence of an earlier Leeds. The respected Venerable Bede talked of a place called 'Leodis' or 'Loidis', long before the Romans landed on our shores. The Romans, it is thought, set up camp just north of the modern day centre. The church at Adel, built by the Normans, stands on the site where the Saxons built before them. There is the Meanwood Valley and Temple Newsam, and the poetic ruins of Kirkstall Abbey set in parkland. They are all evidence of the settlement and the important geographic position of Leeds. How far back do we have to go? Maybe there is no answer, for even words from the language of

The Cottingley bus heading up North Street in 1965.

the Vikings have entered our own language, and with them probably some attitudes. The important thing is that strong feeling of having roots in a place about which one can feel proud. Leeds is certainly such a place. There was real passion and pride when Leeds United were triumphant in the 60s and 70s, and there is heartfelt pain at their defeats, because it is our city that they represent. Leeds is one of the fastest growing cities in Europe. That people of Leeds had the foresight, long ago, to plan for growth. The town developed around the road from the bridge, Briggate, in medieval times. The Victorians realised the importance of transportation for the growth of their industries and linked the city to the coasts by building canals over the Pennines to the west, and developing the navigable river Aire to the sea on the east coast. Modern day planners quickly anticipated the growth of traffic on the roads and planned accordingly. Leeds planners have always been bold and imaginative. Post war building projects were courageous, like 'Queenie's Castle', Quarry Hill Flats, which was very advanced for its time. It required vision to widen the Headrow to create an impressive east to west avenue. The Town Hall, and there are none more grand, was the result of a competition won by a young twenty-nine year old architect from Hull, called Cuthbert Broderick. One cannot help but ask if such responsibility would be risked on someone so young today. And so, reader, turn the pages with care for they contain the heritage built by you and your ancestors. Find all the links that exist between yourselves and the past.

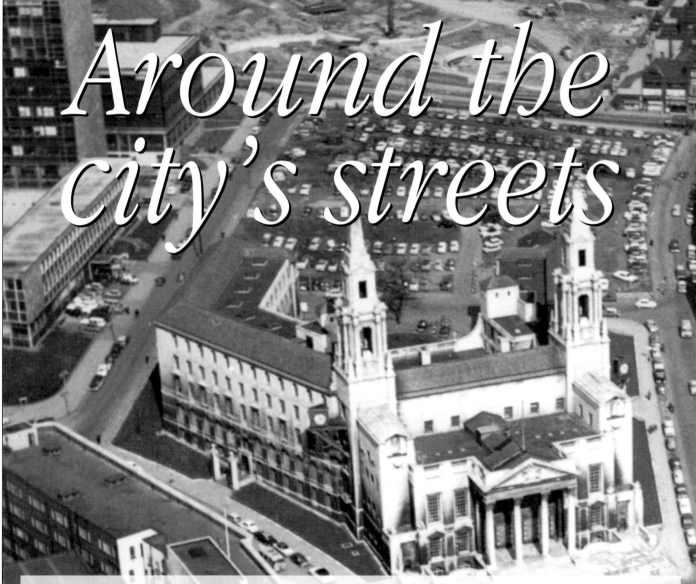

# Around the city's streets

The golden owls, atop the one hundred and seventy feet high twin towers of the Civic Building, are looking down upon one of the fastest growing cities in Europe. This beautiful building, designed by E Vincent Harris, is constructed of Portland stone and took three years to build. It provided work for a large number of unemployed builders and was officially opened by King George V and Queen Mary in August 1933. The year is 1965 and plans are going ahead in the city for a new inner ring road. The land behind the Civic Hall is cleared for some of the many changes that are to follow. Traffic was increasing and moving at much higher speeds. Seat belt anchorage points had to be built into vehicles by the manufacturer by law. By 1983 they were compulsory for all drivers. 'Clunk Click every trip', as Jimmy Savile said in the government information television advert.

To the left can be seen the Brotherton Wing of Leeds General Infirmary. Portland Way leads past the University almost out of our picture in the top left hand corner. In the top right of the picture the white tower block of the Jacob Kramer College of Art dominates the scene. Below is the blackened Leeds Civic Theatre. Originally it was the Leeds Institute of Arts and Sciences, designed by Cuthbert Broderick. Once it was a lecture theatre and, shortly after its' opening, it presented lectures from the famous George Stephenson and, with a bad cold according to reports, the author Charles Dickens. Amongst other more recent 'names', to have 'trod the boards' at the theatre, are Peter O'Toole and Barry Cryer.

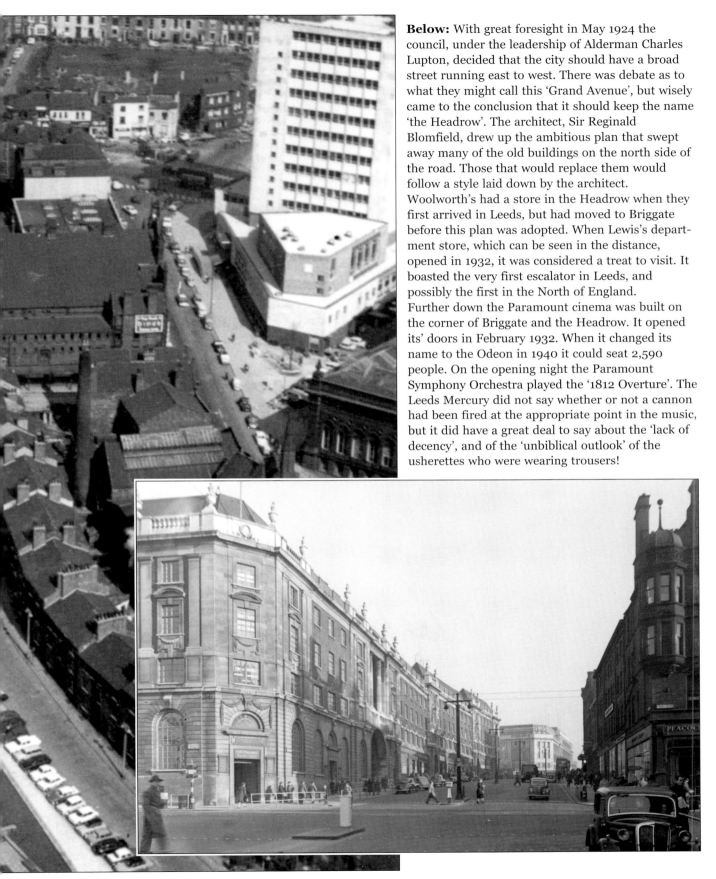

**Below:** With great foresight in May 1924 the council, under the leadership of Alderman Charles Lupton, decided that the city should have a broad street running east to west. There was debate as to what they might call this 'Grand Avenue', but wisely came to the conclusion that it should keep the name 'the Headrow'. The architect, Sir Reginald Blomfield, drew up the ambitious plan that swept away many of the old buildings on the north side of the road. Those that would replace them would follow a style laid down by the architect. Woolworth's had a store in the Headrow when they first arrived in Leeds, but had moved to Briggate before this plan was adopted. When Lewis's department store, which can be seen in the distance, opened in 1932, it was considered a treat to visit. It boasted the very first escalator in Leeds, and possibly the first in the North of England. Further down the Paramount cinema was built on the corner of Briggate and the Headrow. It opened its' doors in February 1932. When it changed its name to the Odeon in 1940 it could seat 2,590 people. On the opening night the Paramount Symphony Orchestra played the '1812 Overture'. The Leeds Mercury did not say whether or not a cannon had been fired at the appropriate point in the music, but it did have a great deal to say about the 'lack of decency', and of the 'unbiblical outlook' of the usherettes who were wearing trousers!

# Events of the 1950s

*WHAT'S ON?*
*Television hit Britain in a big way during the 1950s. Older readers will surely remember 'Double Your Money, Dixon of Dock Green and 'Dragnet' (whose characters' names were changed 'to protect the innocent'). Commercial television was introduced on 22nd September 1955, and Gibbs SR toothpaste were drawn out of the hat to become the first advert to be shown. Many believed adverts to be vulgar, however, and audiences were far less than had been hoped for.*

*GETTING AROUND*
*The year 1959 saw the development of the world's first practical air-cushion vehicle - better known to us as the hovercraft. The earliest model was only able to travel at slow speeds over very calm water and was unable to carry more than three passengers. The faster and smoother alternative to the sea ferry quickly caught on, and by the 1970s a 170-ton car-carrying hover-craft service had been introduced across the English Channel.*

*SPORTING CHANCE*
*The four-minute mile had remained the record since 1945, and had become regarded as virtually unbreakable. On 6th May 1954, however, Oxford University student Roger Bannister literally ran away with the record, accomplishing the seemingly impossible in three min-utes 59.4 seconds. Bannister col-lapsed at the end of his last amaz-ing lap, even temporarily losing his vision. By the end of the day, how-ever, he had recovered sufficiently to celebrate his achievement in a London night club!*

**Above:** Even with the protection of the local bobby, it would be fatal to stand on this spot too long today. In 1956, not only was it possible, one had time to poke a stick into the tramlines, or sweep them with a brush, without fear of being run over. They are not involved in any way with the laying of the trans-Atlantic telephone cable, which was laid at the bottom of the ocean this year, even though it may appear that someone has dug up City Square fairly recently. They are clearing the points so that the trams can change line. They may well never have to do the job again as the trams were

gradually being decommissioned. The Midland bank looks dirty and shrouded in mist, but in this year the Clean-Air Act was passed and came into force two years later. Then many buildings will be cleaned of the grimy sooty deposit to reveal the ornate carvings and statuary that adorn the many elegant buildings of Leeds. The Midland Bank is as grand as any in the city, and, although its' purpose has changed, it still graces the square.

How many remember the Royal Exchange Building on the opposite corner, which is not visible in this picture? The Wine Lodge was always worth a visit, if only to marvel at the large circular Victorian bar, which was as grand and imposing as a Roman amphitheatre.

Flat cloth caps and fawn raincoats were the favoured fashion, with plenty of material in the trousers. The large turn-ups always seemed to be able to catch the dropped silver sixpence, or the three-penny bit, as well as a large amount of fluff and dust.

**Top:** At the end of World War 1, hopefully then termed 'The War to End all Wars', a memorial committee was established in the city to raise funds to erect a suitable memorial to the city's dead. Leeds contributed 90,000 men to the 1914-18 war and 9,640 of them were killed. The worst nightmare occurred on one day on July 1, 1916 when, during the disaster that was the Somme offensive, the Leeds 'Pals', like many, many others, were all but virtually wiped out, losing 750 out of 900 volunteers. The statue was unveiled in City Square in 1922. The figure of Winged Victory hovers above Peace, in the form of a female figure bearing an olive branch, and War, shown as St George slaying the Dragon. Eventually as traffic congestion increased, the memorial was later re-sited on the Headrow's Garden of Remembrance. The history of this war has been depicted in many forms through novels, art, poetry, film and documentary. Not many of these artists and writers or commentators have stated it was a glorious war but prefer to give witness in their own way to the chilling recollections of those who survived or to the equally chilling statistics stating bleakly how many were killed. The recently opened Imperial War Museum in Salford gives many graphic reminders of how that war was really fought and yet the rest of the exhibits in the museum of the history of the world since that time portray very strongly that the lessons from this war were quickly unlearnt, ignored or forgotten.

**Left:** On the 1 March 1956, a 'Feltham' tram 531 makes its' way up Cookridge Street on route 1 to Lawnswood.
The grimy buildings may soon be cleaned and remain that way. The Clean Air Act was passed in this year and would come into force in 1958. Local Authorities could now designate 'smokeless zones'. The coalman could deliver the special smokeless fuel replacement for coal. Some fuel came in the form of a coke. There were also black 'cobs' that looked like cast tar cushions. They burnt away to a fine powder. Very few homes had central heating and relied entirely on the heat from fires for warmth. No one wanted to get out of bed on a winter's morning until Dad had a reasonable fire burning. Everyone had to learn the skill of rolling newspapers around a knitting needle to form a 'stick'. It was then looped to form a ring. These would burn long enough to get the fuel ignited.
With the introduction of 'Baxi' fires, the fire could be regulated. The air was brought through a tube from beneath the floor and could be controlled with a 'butterfly flap' valve. The fire burnt very fiercely when the valve was fully open.
Further up the road in Rossington Street, is the Leeds School of Art, where a Liverpool lad was a student. He was, however,

to become better known for his ability to kick his leg in the air whilst asking for 'the moonlight' and 'a girl', and we could then 'leave the rest' to him. His name was Frankie Abelson, who changed it to Frankie Vaughan.

**Above:** On the corner of Cross Park Street and Park Row, known better as Victoria Square, Hood's Travel Office can let you fly around the world with BOAC or, more usual for most, provide a railway ticket to Filey, Scarborough or Bridlington. During the 'textile' weeks, or the 'engineering' weeks, when the factories closed, families packed their suitcases and headed for their favourite boarding house, where the landlady would greet them by name once a year. The gentleman, standing outside Hood's, seems to be trying to make up his mind, whilst others rush past too quick for the camera shutter. He may be thinking about Prime Minister Harold McMillan's words, 'Most of our people have never had it so good.' He may be wondering if he is one of the 'most'. If the cost of a holiday is beyond his means, there are lots of parks and walks within easy reach of the city centre and Vince's shop can provide a pair of boots, at a reasonable price, or

repair his old ones to look like new. He may decide to take up a hobby instead for a little further along is the Yorkshire training College of Music.

No double yellow lines or traffic wardens. Not even a parking meter. Parking meters were an idea imported from America. It seems like poetic justice that the first ones in England were erected outside the American Embassy in London.

**Top:** The Headrow, that Grand Avenue of Leeds, was originally conceived by Sir Reginald Blomfield in 1925. Luckily the people of Leeds have been able to keep the spirit of his original vision throughout the years. Lewis's department store opened in the Headrow in 1932. Amongst these imposing facades, on the left, is a narrow entrance, which might easily be overlooked by a stranger to the city, but they would certainly know it better than any other building in the area if they were told that it is the 'City Palace of Varieties'. It began life as the 'White Swan', which is now called 'Barney's'. It was built in the eighteenth century as a coaching inn, to which a singing room was added. A hundred years later Thornton's New Music Hall was built above it. In 1953 the BBC television programme 'The Good Old Days' was filmed there. Its producer, Barney Colehan, now gives his name to the establishment in Swan Street. During the 30s there was a man called Jenkinson who was the chairman of the housing committee. As well as developing the centre, he wanted to improve living conditions for the poorer people of the city. From 1933 onwards he lead a campaign to clear away slums and provide better housing. Before people were allowed to move into the new houses their furniture had to be passed through a defestation van filled with gas. The van was affectionately christened 'Jenkinson's bug van'. Some of the houses, which were built at that time, had bay windows. They were called 'sunshine houses', and were usually allocated to families with one or more members diagnosed as needing more than usual light and fresh air because of poor health.

The lorry rumbling up Briggate past Queens Arcade may, or may not be, an army vehicle. Lots of ex-army vehicles were sold for civilian use after the war. Although a one-way street in 1967, they certainly wouldn't be moving in this direction today. Drivers would have found the deliberate narrowing of a roadway to slow vehicles down, and at the priority now given to pedestrians, quite amazing. Massive changes were taking place on the roads around Leeds in 1967. The ring road was being cut and many buildings were sacrificed in order that the traffic could move more easily. The general public were allowed to walk through the one thousand two hundred foot tunnel section of the inner ring road. The Mayor of Leeds, Alderman J S Walsh, performed the official opening on 14th January 1967. The minister of transport that year was Barbara Castle. The shops are now full, and the war is but a memory. It is possible to buy a stereophonic music centre with a record player, radio, two speakers, and a tape recorder that operated tape cassettes. Some machines could be set to take either the old 78rpm records or the newer 33s!s, and would drop the pick-up arm automatically! Records could be stacked as many as six at a time. What will they think of next? It was possible to have hours of continuous playing of Beatles records, much to the joy of parents. When the Beatles were discovered, many a father, like one major recording company, declared that they were a passing 'fad' that would never catch on! They were both wrong.

independent borough until 1974 in the old West Riding when it became under the umbrella of the mammoth city of Leeds yet, like many of these enlarged communities, it retained its identity. It is still Horsforth.

**Left:** Children skip and play while their parents wait for the tram on route 6 to Meanwood. The photographer must have been standing at the end of Barrack Street. Maybe he was enjoying the 'satisfaction' promised on the poster as he smoked his Senior Service Cigarette. It was fashionable to smoke then, and no one seemed to connect the habit with lung cancer. Perhaps smokers preferred 'Digger' tobacco, or St. Bruno, with its strong aroma. As well as the usual packets of ten or twenty, it was possible to buy Woodbines in paper packets of five for a nine pence halfpenny. Many a boy, and some girls, acquired the habit with these little 'coffin nails'. Sitting in the dark air-raid shelter in the recreation ground, and telling stories around the light of a candle, the evil little cigarette would circulate. Our Persil white shirts would not remain noticeably brighter after playing in there. The adverts always made mothers feel that they were somehow failing their families if they did not make the washing brighter than the next door neighbour's. Some washing powders had blue speckles in them to give that extra 'brightness'. Just like the 'Dolly Blue' on a stick used by grandmothers. Children collected things then, like Bass bottle tops with the triangular motif as seen on the poster. There were different colours for different beers. We had collections of cigarette cards and swapped them in the school playground. We were experts in identifying the rare ones, and jealously clung to the silk ones mother had saved when she was a girl.

**Top:** After the second world war Leeds set about building new residential districts or enlarging by house building existing communities as part of its slum clearance programme. New estates meant new roads as they cut across other main roads, hence the need for roundabouts and dual carriageways. However demand often exceeded supply and Leeds like many other cities always seemed to be catching up. You would not think that this ring road was designed to ease traffic congestion but it was and it was necessary. This 1960s photograph of the ring road at Horsforth does give an idea of the size of the project. One effect it did have was to bring communities like Horsforth 'closer' to the city. Horsforth became a suburb whereas it was previously thought of as a self sufficient little town. It had an abundance of churches, parks and recreation areas. There were schools, the Glenroyal cinema, local shopping, sports clubs and pubs a plenty. Who needed to go to Leeds except for a day out? But new estates brought an influx of people from the city. Horsforth grew and grew and grew. It even managed to survive as an

# *Events & occasions*

How young these trainee nurses look as they take part in the Ark Royal parade in May 1942. Times were difficult and there was little time to be young. As soon as they were out of school they were involved in responsible work for the war effort. Looking at the sisters or matrons, one gets the impression that only the best efforts and highest standards from the girls will be acceptable. They were like the Sergeant Major in that respect. Soldiers believed that the 'sarge' was the secret weapon that would sway the outcome of the war. We had to win because he would not accept anything short of that aim. Prior to the war a woman's place was in the home, but now they were working on the land in their familiar khaki uniform of the land girl. The city lass learned how to milk a cow and plough a field. The only men who were exempt from the armed forces were the farmers themselves who were classified as 'essential workers' in 'reserved occupations'. The women of Britain were operating lathes in the factory producing guns and ammunition. There was nothing they could not do. They delivered the daily 'pinta' and, not only did they collect the fares on the buses, but they drove the buses as well. Some involved themselves in Civil Defence, and others joined the Women's Voluntary Service. There was little chance that these determined women would slip quietly back into the role they had had before the war.

The Scots Regiment take the lead as the cadets swing around the corner from Albion Street into Victoria Square. Everyone loves the stirring music of a military band, and particularly when it is played for the joy of victory, and the end of such a war. 'Is it true that they wear nothing beneath their kilts, Ethel?' 'I don't know, but I do know that the Prime Minister says we shall have to continue making our own from any available bits of material. He says that rationing will have to continue. I know that I am glad of a bit of parachute silk to make certain garments, which decency prevents me from mentioning'. The ladies were wonderful at saving those bits of material, from blackout curtains or from any other source. Granny used to wind up any bits of string from parcels into balls and place them carefully into the kitchen drawer with the remark, 'Don't you know there is a war on?' There were valuable lessons to be learned about wasting nothing. We ate everything put on our plates. Food was rationed. There was little sugar but the children liked to watch the tiny saccharin tablets foam as they dissolved in mum's tea. 'Woman's Hour' gave wondrous recipes for making Carrot Jam and eggless cakes. The government extolled the virtues of carrots. They helped you to see in the dark of the blackout, or so the comedians of the time would have us believe. 'You've never seen a rabbit wearing glasses!'

# Events of the 1940s

*WHAT'S ON?*
*In wartime Britain few families were without a wireless set. It was the most popular form of entertainment, and programmes such as ITMA, Music While You Work and Workers' Playtime provided the people with an escape from the harsh realities of bombing raids and ration books. In 1946 the BBC introduced the Light Programme, the Home Service and the Third Programme, which gave audiences a wider choice of listening.*

*GETTING AROUND*
*October 1948 saw the production of Britain's first new car designs since before the war. The Morris Minor was destined for fame as one of the most popular family cars, while the four-wheel-drive Land Rover answered the need for a British-made off-road vehicle.*
*The country was deeply in the red, however, because of overseas debts incurred during the war. The post-war export drive that followed meant that British drivers had a long wait for their own new car.*

*SPORTING CHANCE*
*American World Heavyweight Boxing Champion Joe Louis, who first took the title back in 1937, ruled the world of boxing during the 1930s and 40s, making a name for himself as unbeatable. Time after time he successfully defended his title against all comers, finally retiring in 1948 after fighting an amazing 25 title bouts throughout his boxing career. Louis died in 1981 at the age of 67.*

**Above:** We saluted them, in May 1945, as they marched down the Headrow. The war in Europe was over. On the previous day people had huddled around their radios to listen to the King give one of his first broadcasts since being crowned, and to Winston Churchill announcing an end to the war. The King had always had a nervous stutter, but there was no sign of that impediment on this day. 'The shadow has passed', he said, 'let us remember those who will not come back - they are not with us at the moment of rejoicing.' The BBC Home Service had announced a 'Victory Programme'. It would begin, they said, with 'lift up your hearts', at 7.55 am, followed by 'Robinson Cleaver at the organ', at 10 am, and a 'Works Concert' at mid-day. The Prime Minister would address the Nation at 3

**Top:** The ladies of the WRNS, keen to show that they are as smart and as well trained as their male counter-parts, march proudly down Boar Lane on this day in June 1944. It was a parade to 'Salute the Soldier', but they too were being saluted, by this well dressed and very orderly crowd. There was no need for a large police presence to control this multitude. They dressed in their best, and turned out in their hundreds. The ladies had put their hair in rag rollers the night before, and pinned it in place ready for the day. Their hats made a statement about their status and personality. There were homburgs and flat caps, like the one Andy Cap wore in the newspaper cartoon strip. There were ladies' felt hats, some with flamboyant feathers, and there were knitted bonnets, as well as a few military hats and berets. The procession was lead by the Band of the West Yorkshire Regiment pumping out stirring music. Royal Navy Officers and Ratings followed the band. The WRNS and the Royal Artillery, who brought some anti-aircraft guns with them, followed next. Bands of the Northamptonshire Regiment added to the excitement. There were Army Cadets, Civil Defence Messengers, and a rear guard of ex-servicemen of the British Legion. It was a sight to make a person feel proud to be British. The people responded and raised almost £7 million; well above the intended target of £5 million.

pm. Crowds in the streets fell silent as Churchill's speech was broadcast. He told them of how General Jodl had signed an unconditional surrender. He reminded the people that the war in the East was not yet over, but ended with the words, 'Advance Brittania. Long live freedom. God save the King.' The streets exploded as the crowds cheered and burst into song.

In London the people stood in front of Buckingham palace and shouted for 'Winnie. He came out onto the balcony with the King and Queen. Churchill was, of course, the man of the moment.

'All the nice girls love a sailor' in the words of the song - and it seems to be true. Or is it that they are caught up in the euphoria of the celebration for the end of war with Japan? Is it simply a pose for the camera as the photographer records history in Albion Street on the sixteenth of August 1945? Whatever the reason, Jack Tar is going to grin and bear it! The enormity of the 'new kind of bomb' that the Americans had dropped on Japan and the effect it was to have on the world was not yet clear. The news travelled slowly and we would have to wait for the cock to crow on the Cinema Pathe News, or for reports to filter through to the radio stations and the newspapers.

For now the boys have applied a good coating of Brylcreem to their hair, and checked with care to see that the parting is straight. Combed it back, then, pushing with the flat of the hand, twisted it forwards to form a waving quiff. Mum always covered the backs of the chairs with antimacassars to prevent them from acquiring a greasy stain. She made them look attractive with the addition of a crocheted edge.

If that is a ration book, which the young lady on the right is clutching, and she has any thoughts of destroying the horrid thing, she had better think again. The war may be at an end, but things were to get worse before getting better and rationing would continue for a few years yet.

**Left:** The lions on the town hall steps supported revellers looking for a good vantage point to watch all the goings on. This was VJ day in August 1945. They had done the same when Victory was gained in Europe, and VE day had been declared a public holiday. Now, after the  Americans had dropped a second atomic bomb, Japan had surrendered. Weren't the ladies glad that they had turned themselves out in their best? Felt hats were brushed; old coats had been given a 'make do and mend' new lease of life with the addition of a little lace or a fur collar. Headscarves were quite acceptable, after all the Princesses and the Queen occasionally wore them. Some preferred to have no headwear at all so that their wavy quiffs, held in place with a little Brylcreem no doubt, could been seen. The war may be at an end, and there is cause for celebration, but very soon after Britain's new Prime Minister, Clement Attlee, would bring the people back to reality with a warning that there was no likelihood of immediate prosperity. They would have to suffer rationing for a few more years to come. They would not be able to buy new clothes without carefully counting their coupons.

**Below:** Schools were closed. Shops, offices and factories gave their workers a holiday for the war in Japan was ended. This was VJ Day! For many the celebrations for VE Day had been premature, for, although there was a victory in Europe, their loved ones were still away in the East involved in the conflict there. The people of Leeds, as did people all over the land, went out and danced in the streets. Outside the town Hall they waltzed with joy. Never mind the rain, a headscarf, felt hat, or that hood that buttoned behind the coat collar will keep off the rain. On the sixth August 1945 the war with Japan had been brought to a terrifying conclusion. An American B29 Super Fortress bomber, named 'The Enola Gay' after the captain's mother, dropped a 'Little Boy' on Hiroshima. The 'Little Boy' was the first design atomic bomb, which developed into 'Fat Man' by its inventor J Robert Oppenheimer. 'Fat Man' was dropped on Nagasaki three days later. The Japanese surrendered. More than one hundred thousand were killed and thousands injured for life. No war would ever be the same again.

**Below:** August 14 1945 proved to be a most significant day in the history of World War 2 as Japan surrendered after the United States unleashed atomic bombs on the cities of Nagasaki and Hiroshima and by the next day it was all over. Victory had been achieved in Europe some months earlier and the celebrations then were countrywide. The VJ celebrations were not as boisterous as those on VE day but no doubt just as welcome. Men were still returning from the war though there are a significant number here in this photograph. Leeds had suffered lightly compared to other British cities with the official numbers being 77 civilians dead and 327 injured. 197 buildings were destroyed and there were nine air raids. But that was in the past now. The 'V' sign and the smiles of the residents of the Manor Grove area say it all. The street party was for the children of course but it is interesting here how many men are present no doubt having returned from service. There are reminders here of the last few years in the brick built air raid shelters and a chilling thought that the wheelchair victim might have been a wounded soldier. As on many great and significant occasions each person will have a story to tell about the parties, the fun and mostly the relief that war was a thing of the past. Now was the time to plan for the future. No more threats of bombs, no more blackouts. But some things will go on for a little longer. Rationing!

For the residents of Park Street, as for everyone in the land, there was much to celebrate on VE day. There was Victory in Europe, and soon their sons, fathers and husbands would be home for good. There would no longer be any need to hide even the smallest chink of light from enemy bombers. The lamppost could be lit, and the white stripe painted around it could be removed. The young men standing beneath it will still be called up for National Service, which will not end for another decade, but at least they will not be shot at or bombed. What they dreaded more than such an enemy, was the army barber. In partnership with the Sergeant Major, they would make sure that the wavy quiffs of hair would be sacrificed for King and Country, and that 'short back and sides' would become the order of the day. But for today, forget 'call up', rationing, or the blackout which has now gone, and bring the benches from the chapel, and the chairs from the kitchen. Prop any old doors not used to bridge between the tables against the railings, and party in the cobbled Park Street. Dress in your best, displaying your talents in 'make do and mend', but protect them with a flowered apron. Manufacture some party hats from anything you can find. Show what can be done with eggs from granddad's bantam hens, a little flower and powdered milk, mixed with your precious sugar ration. To complete the recipe for joy, sing songs about 'bluebirds over the White Cliffs of Dover', or lights going on all over the world.

**Above:** 'God save the Queen' is the message of the day, as Leeds gets ready to celebrate the coronation in style. A stage is set for speeches, music and singing, and the sun is shining. Unfortunately the weather was not so good for the Coronation on 2nd June 1953. It was a cold and rainy day, but the splendour of the event was not dampened by the weather. Everyone followed the route from maps printed in their daily newspapers. The positions of the static television cameras were clearly marked. The cameras were large and had to be mounted on huge metal carriers. The commentators broadcast all they could before the Golden coach, drawn by eight white horses, went out of sight of their cameras. They then passed on to a colleague and the image switched to the next stage along the way to the abbey. Most children knew the changes in designs of the decorations along the royal route. Each section had a particular theme. Models of the coronation coach were on sale in the shops. The whole nation was, for the first time in history, fully involved in the coronation of their monarch. The flags of St George surround the War Memorial in the Garden of Rest, on which there is a magnificent statue of the saint cast in bronze. Designed by H C Fehr, the memorial used to stand in City Square, near the Majestic cinema, but was moved in front of the Art Gallery in 1937.

**Right:** The year is, of course, 1953. With such a name the Queen's Arcade, is the right place to celebrate the crowning of a new queen, Elizabeth II. Once upon a time this was the site of the Rose and Crown coaching Inn, equally appropriately named for a coronation celebration. It was one of several such inns in this area, and stagecoaches ran from here to Hull and London on a regular basis. Maybe this was one of the inns, as the story goes, in which the highwayman, Dick Turpin, used to gather information and planned his robberies. The arcade was built in 1889 and was designed by a London architect, Edward Clark. Around the balcony, behind the wrought iron railings, is another row of shops. There are several beautiful arcades of which the first to be opened was Thornton's. This too was built on the site of another coaching in, the Talbot. The Talbot was the inn where jockeys met to be weighed before going to the Leeds racecourse on Chapeltown Moor.

Leeds, it seems, was well ahead of its' times in providing pedestrianised shopping areas. There are many items of interest to be seen in the windows of the Queen's Arcade today. The gentleman maybe wondering if he can afford to buy a television so that he, and his family, can watch the Coronation live from London. Or maybe he will simply accept the kind invitation to go next door to watch. Sales of televisions rocketed in preparation for the longest live broadcast ever televised.

# Events of the 1950s

*HOT OFF THE PRESS*
*The 1950s seemed to be the heyday of spies, and in 1951 the activities of Guy Burgess and Donald Maclean caused a sensation in the country. Both had occupied prominent positions in the Foreign Office, while Burgess had also been a member of MI-6. Recruited by the Russians while at Cambridge University in the 1930s, the traitors provided the Soviets with a huge amount of valuable information. They disappeared in 1951, surfacing in Moscow five years later.*

*THE WORLD AT LARGE*
*Plans to develop the economies of member states into one common market came to fruition on 1st January 1958, when the EEC came into operation. The original members were France, Belgium, Luxembourg, The Netherlands, Italy, and West Germany. The Community became highly successful, achieving increased trade and prosperity across Western Europe while at the same time alleviating fear of war which lingered on after the end of World War II. Britain became a member in 1973.*

*ROYAL WATCH*
*King George VI's health had been causing problems since 1948, when he developed thrombosis. In 1951 the King - always a heavy smoker - became ill again, and was eventually found to be suffering from lung cancer. His left lung was removed in September of 1951. In January 1952 he waved Princess Elizabeth and Prince Philip off on their tour of Africa; they were never to see him again. The King died on 5th February 1952.*

**Below:** Who are these young ladies? They must remember the day when they were photographed in City Square in 1953. There are certain dates which, when mentioned in conversation, elicit the response, 'I remember where I was, and who I was with, and what we were doing when that happened'. It could be the assassination of a president or the crowning of a queen, but such happenings are etched firmly into our minds, and act as our own historic markers. We remember being given our coronation mugs in school, or our copies of the New Testament, even if we cannot remember what happened to them in the years that followed. It is a medieval theme that has been chosen for the square's decorations, with banners and lances ready for the joust. The Black Prince is just out of the picture, but he is probably smiling now, for he would surely approve. It has always been a puzzle to the people of Leeds why Colonel Harding chose the Black Prince as the subject for a statue by Thomas Brock, as the prince had no apparent connection with the city. It is, however, a fine equestrian bronze that greets all those who walk from the station with a dignified presence. Those who were unable to witness the coronation on television, could watch highlights of the event at the News Theatre, by the station entrance, during the following week.

**Inset:** The News Theatre, and the station entrance, are decorated for the forthcoming coronation. The theatre used to present hour long programmes of news, cartoons, and travelogues, to keep travellers entertained, whilst they waited for their train. It also provided courting couples a warm shelter from the rain and the romance of the

darkness, for the sum of sixpence. A shilling paid for the more private back seats. The programme repeated every hour from twelve noon until eleven at night. The sale of televisions, with their small tinted screens, rocketed as those who could afford prepared to witness the coronation in the comfort of their own sitting rooms. Neighbours were invited in and served with sandwiches cut into triangles, with all the crust removed. This was an obvious sign that their hosts were middle class, if the ownership of a television had not already conveyed that message. Throughout the longest continuous television programme ever recorded, Granny could not comprehend that we were witnessing the event as it unfolded and kept asking, 'When was the Queen crowned?' The News Theatre would not receive the film for a few days, by which time most of the population would know about it through the magic of television.

Cinemas were already struggling for survival, and the News Theatre had shown the first ever 'Art Film', given an 'X' (adult only) rating, only the previous year. Usually in French or Italian, these films were dubbed, or had sub-titles printed along the bottom of the screen, and were very 'saucy'! The 'News Theatre' became the 'Classic', and then the 'Tatler Film Club', and later changed back to the 'Classic', before eventually closing in 1983.

**Below:** This 1958 visit by the royal couple was indeed a tremendous occasion. A young Queen and her dashing husband made an ideal pairing as the country continued its re-growth after the turmoil of the Second World War. Here the royal party is been driven up the Headrow with the crowds straining to catch a glimpse of their majesties. The necessary formality of the visit had been observed. At the Town Hall there were the formal presentations to civic dignitaries, inspections of guards of honour, speeches of welcome and thanks and all the ritual that a royal visit would bring. The people of Leeds gathered in their thousands to greet the Queen hours before the ceremonies began. The staff and patients of Brotherton Wing of Leeds General Infirmary had used every vantage point to secure the best possible view of the proceedings and what a view they would have had overlooking the forecourt of the Town Hall. No walkabout there though. That was years ahead. And yet the need for the strict security that was evident here was not as necessary as it is today. The only danger to the Queen here would have been over enthusiasm as the crowds surged and ran forward to snatch a fleeting glimpse. Many would have gone home totally convinced the Queen or the Duke had specially waved to them, while others more fortunate would remember for years that they met and shook hands with or even presented a bouquet to the Queen.

**Above:** No VIP visit to Leeds would have been complete without a visit to Burton's factory. Chairman, Lionel Jacobson is here escorting Her Majesty the Queen passing through an avenue of highly excited shop floor workers may of whom wore colourful favours in their hair. All departments had been decorated with yards and yards of red, white and blue trimmings. Coffee had been served to the Queen and the Duke of Edinburgh. This visit 5 years after the Queen's coronation took place as the factory was at its prosperous height. Its Hudson Road Mills claimed to be the world's biggest tailoring workshop and offered an impressive array of facilities which included a doctor, a nurse, an optician, a dentist, chiropodist, sick benefit, sun-ray equipment and sports facilities and no town or city was complete without the famous Montague Burton shop front  Sir Montague Burton himself explained it quite simply when he stated 'A man's general bearing becomes more confident when he is well dressed'. Pioneering of course. A royal visit at this time had less of the informality than they have today. No walkabout here but there are signs that the Queen is actually enjoying and appreciating the welcome she is given. After all there were very few homes with television so glimpses of the Queen and the royal family were confined to newspapers and magazines at he cinema with Pathe news. Real life visits were few and far between and for the employees of Burtons this particular occasion was well worth savouring and celebrating.

**Top right:** As the Royal visitors, the Queen and Prince Phillip drive through Leeds during the Queen's Jubilee year 1977, every available vantage point is taken. Even the rooftops are taken by loyal subjects wishing for a spectacular view. The crowd are orderly, but enthusiastic, as the Royal car drives slowly down the avenue of cadets stood smartly to attention. Some spectators have clambered up the war memorial in order to see above the heads of the gathered crowd. H C Fehr's winged statue is completely hidden. The war memorial was moved from city square to its' present site, in front of the Art Gallery, in 1937. When the Queen's uncle abdicated, her father became king, and that changed her life also. The spotlight now fell on her, even more than it had done in the past. The young princess knew that, one day, she would carry this great burden of responsibility. She had been out of the country on a tour in place of her father, the King, who was too ill to go himself, when the news was received of his death. He had suffered from cancer for a number of years. Prince Phillip had the unenviable task of breaking the news to her. In her jubilee year the people were expressing their admiration for the way in which she had carried out her role over twenty-five glorious years.

**Right:** The band played stirring music as the Queen and the Duke of Edinburgh were warmly welcomed. The celebrations, held at the football ground to celebrate her Jubilee, were in full swing. The streets on the way to the stadium had been lined with loyal well-wishers, and there was a real party atmosphere. The 'pawns', the 'white knight', and all of the black 'chess-pieces' must have been feeling warm, and maybe a little itchy, in their splendid costumes. To many of the adults assembled here it did not seem like

twenty-five years since she had become their queen.
Many could remember being giving a coronation
mug, many of which did not arrive home in one
piece, or a copy of the New Testament with an
inscription stamped on the cover. Children had been
given the day off school, twenty-five years ago, to
watch the marathon television broadcast of the event.
The longest continual live broadcast ever. How young
the Queen looked as the Archbishop lowered the
crown onto her head. It was such a responsibility.
Just as they, who had not forgotten the coronation
celebrations, the children and everyone else waving
their flags in the crowd, would remember this day,
and the feeling of national pride, forever. Was any
reader there on that day? Were you a 'chess piece'?

# *At leisure*

E veryone of a certain age will have his or her own memories of the Queen's Coronation in June 1953. Many watched the whole day on a black and white television. There were street parties, carnivals bonfires. It was a day to celebrate the official recognition of a new monarch. No one could ignore it. Every part of the country had its own way of celebrating. One common link was that every child received a coronation mug. These young men in this photograph from the Quarry Hill estate will now be fathers and grandfathers and it would be interesting to see if they remember the festivities and in fact if they have kept their mugs. After the Second World War the Quarry Hill residents had made conscious efforts to create a sense of community. A tenants' association had been formed with an annual carnival being one of the highlights. These carnivals were all day affairs beginning in the morning with a procession of as many as 20 floats and events lasting until late evening. The interest was not just confined to the estate. It became a red-letter day in the city's social calendar. The Festival of Britain in 1951 had been another opportunity to foster this spirit. Again a Carnival was held with a Carnival Queen elected. A Fancy Dress competition attracted 500 children's entries. So the 1953 Coronation gave the residents of Quarry Hill another chance to celebrate with games, competitions and to complete the day a children's concert.

# Events of the 1950s

*SCIENCE AND DISCOVERY*
*DNA (deoxyribonucleic acid) was first defined as long ago as 1953, and the effects have been far-reaching. The key discovery was developed over the following years and today DNA fingerprinting has become an accepted part of life. Genetic diseases such as haemophilia and cystic fibrosis have been identified. Criminals are continually detected and brought to justice. Biological drugs have been developed. More controversially, drought and disease-resistant plants have been engineered - and Dolly the sheep has been produced.*

*MELODY MAKERS*
*Few teenage girls could resist the blatant sex-appeal of 'Elvis the Pelvis', though their parents were scandalised at the moody Presley's provocatively gyrating hips. The singer took America and Britain by storm with such hits as 'Jailhouse Rock', 'All Shook Up' and 'Blue Suede Shoes'. The rhythms of Bill Haley and his Comets, Buddy Holly, Chuck Berry, and Roy Orbison (who had a phenomenal three-octave voice) turned the 1950s into the Rock 'n' Roll years.*

*INVENTION AND TECHNOLOGY*
*Until the late 1950s you did not carry radios around with you. Radios were listened to at home, plugged into a mains socket in every average sitting room. Japan was in the forefront of electronic developments even then, and in 1957 the Japanese company Sony introduced the world's very first all-transistor radio - an item of new technology that was small enough to fit into your pocket. The major consumer product caught on fast - particularly with teenage listeners.*

**Above:** Is this a picture of rural England? Is it some village green in the heart of the countryside, where the local residents are waiting for the bowling match to begin? The answer to both questions is, 'No'. It is in the centre of busy Leeds. It is just one of the beautiful backwaters to be discovered amidst the river of people and traffic. There is nothing to shatter the peace on this bright sunny day in May 1955. 'Graffiti' and 'vandalism' seem not to have entered our vocabulary yet, but soon there will be a whole host of words and sounds to change the world forever. 'Teenagers' will be invented. 'Rock and Roll', we will be told, is 'here to stay'. Cinemas will be torn apart as young people dance in the isles and pull up chairs to make more room to dance to the music of a round-faced American musician with a 'kiss curl' on his

**Top:** The Clock cinema in Harehills was aptly named. It could have been called the Fountain for there was one in the foyer as well as a foyer, a café and a parade of shops. But 'Clock' was obvious. This Art Deco building was opened in 1938 with 'The Hurricane' starring the glamorous Dorothy Lamour and its final showing in 1976 was, aptly, 'The Incredible Journey'. Cinemas before and after the Second World War were vital parts of people's social lives. They were called picture palaces and had a name like Picturedrome. They had wide staircases, candelabras, organs and some even had a resident orchestra. Think of the names of these palaces of the screen, names like Royalty, Regent, Rex, Majestic, Carlton, Ritz, Savoy and Palais. Crossgates in Leeds had a Regal cinema which actually did live up to its name. These names give the impression of grandness. What impression would the Lounge in Headingley give or the Easy or the Cottage or the Pavilion? Homely and relaxing places, hopefully, to forget the cares of the world and immerse oneself in a celluloid world in Arizona, Morocco or the other exotic places that Hollywood could create. Some cinema names were unusually unique like the Alhambra or the Gaiety. Others were hard to decipher. What does Roxy mean? Where did Odeon or Gaumont originate? What is or was Essoldo? Hippodrome in France means something unconnected with the cinema. Which of these cinemas or names now survive? Many like the Clock serve another purpose. They are nightclubs or bingo halls or furniture or electrical stores. What has replaced them? Screen 1, Screen 2. Where is the glamour and romance in that?

forehead. Bill Haley and his Comets when they appear in the film 'Blackboard Jungle'. This rebellious film will be banned in cinemas in many towns to protect decent folk from its' influence. But their song, 'Rock Around the Clock', topped the charts for many months. In the following year it became the title of another controversial film.

As Britain recovered from the effects of the war years, people wanted their High Fidelity music players. They wanted to turn up the music and dance. They had faced the years of austerity and now entered the years of 'live now - pay later', or the 'never-never' as some called hire purchase.

# A man of many parts

Cars are made from an awful lot of parts. And when one of them goes wrong it is crucial to be able to get hold of the right replacement as quickly as possible. Fortunately garages, dealers, exhaust and repair outlets know exactly who to contact: the Leeds-based firm of Andrew Page Ltd, a company which stocks no fewer than 70,000 different parts and can deliver any one of them within an hour.

The name Andrew Page first appeared in the Leeds area in 1917 when James' father, Andrew Page, started a business, later called Andrew Page & Son, with premises at 94 Albion Street, describing himself as a wholesale motor accessories merchant.

These were the early days of car travel when the motor car still a novelty for most people and a time when owning a car was something only the wealthy could consider. But though the market was still relatively small the market was still there, and those who did own motor vehicles inevitably had need of accessories to go with them. Not surprisingly in those days of open topped vehicles the firm sold car rugs, drivers' coats, gloves, goggles, caps, boots, tools and a limited range of components such as spark plugs, horns and lights.

In the 1920s, following a visit to America where the modern car industry had been born, the business began importing some of the very first hydraulic jacks and lifts from the USA. Andrew Page set up a separate London-based subsidiary company, Service Equipment Ltd, to handle that expanding side of the business whilst Leeds-

***Above left****: Andrew Page, founder of the original Andrew Page & Son Limited.* ***Below:*** *An early view of the type of garage equipment available from Andrew Page & Son Ltd.*

based Epco Tools, another Page family firm, began to manufacture items of garage equipment under licence.

Andrew Page died in 1927, not living to witness the disaster and later triumph which would be his legacy; for a time the company continued to slowly expand but eventually had to close its doors, going in to liquidation in the early years of the second world war when the supply of car components dried up as imports were halted by German U-boats and UK manufacturers switched all their production facilities to the war effort.

The company which exists today came into being on 21st June 1946 with the name Andrew Page & Co Ltd. The new company was set up by Jim Page, the son of the late Andrew Page. Jim Page decided to use his late father's name as it was already known in the motor industry, and at the back of his mind he hoped he might one day have a son whom he would name Andrew after his father.

Before the second world war began Jim Page had worked for his father's company, learning his trade by working in the warehouse, serving on at the counter and running errands.

Because he had enjoyed the work it was natural for Jim to try and emulate his father's success and revive his business after leaving the army at the end of the war.

Jim had joined the Royal Artillery as soon as the prospect of war became imminent. Initially he was stationed at a training camp at Pateley Bridge, North Yorkshire and six months later went up to Iceland where he spent the next twelve months living in freezing conditions. Expecting to be next posted to Europe he was sent home on leave for 10 days and then was told, in typical army fashion, that he would be joining an Indian regiment. The rest of Jim's war was spent as Captain of the Royal Artillery in the sweltering heat of India and Ceylon, bolstering the Empire's defences against the Japanese.

Jim re-started the business with his army gratuity of £800. To begin with the new company could not pay any wages so Jim earned the money to look after his home and his wife by

*Top*: *The well equipped shop gets the business, something Andrew Page can still boast today.*
*Above*: *A company invoice from 1923.*

buying a second hand car each Thursday evening, spending Friday evening cleaning and polishing it and then, hopefully, selling it at a profit on a Saturday - something which he would keep on doing until 1953.

When Jim Page had set up the new company he also took on a partner, his cousin Ken Purchon who had also earlier worked for Andrew Page & Son: it was a perfect partnership. Jim Page did the selling and the buying whilst Ken Purchon handled all the administration and looked after the warehouse. It would be two years before any other staff were employed: the first office employee would be Jim's wife Joan.

The business started off by selling vehicle starter batteries and shock absorbers from premises at 68 Albion Street: new product was however very difficult to get immediately after the war and both these items had to be repaired or remanufactured.

The batteries were from a company called Chloride and the shock absorbers from Armstrong, a Hull-based firm. Business was slow as the country was still getting over the long war and the number of private cars on the road was only a fraction of what they are today.

Eventually however other products followed the re-conditioned batteries and shock absorbers, products such as Girling brakes and Bosch electrical parts, an arrangement which began in 1947 when the firm was invited to become a Bosch distributor.

The partnership had become a limited liability company in 1947 under the name Andrew Page & Co Ltd with Jim Page and Ken Purchon as its directors. During that year car radios appeared on their shelves for the first time whilst another company Service Equipment (Leeds) Ltd was registered by them, reviving another part of the earlier business.

By the mid 1950s the company was growing sufficiently for larger premises to be sought; in 1955 it moved to Millwright Street in Leeds 2.

The following year with Service Equipment (Leeds) Ltd having been appointed as Girling brakes and shock absorber distributors trading began at 71/73 Roseville Road, Leeds 8; Lockheed brake service, clutches and exhaust systems were now added to the range whilst HM Gorman, who, in 1969, would become a director, now joined the team.

***Top****: Garage equipment.*
***Above****: A 1928 statement.*

The year of 1957 saw the opening of the first branch when premises were purchased in Market Street, Wakefield, from a brakes company Small and Parks which was run by Peter Wood who is still working within the company. This branch was opened to handle sales in South Yorkshire.

Back in Leeds, in the next year, Andrew Page & Co began trading from 53/59 Mabgate Leeds 9 on the site of what would eventually become famous as Apson House, the hub of a massive business. A second branch would open in Harrogate in 1963 to service North Yorkshire.

Bob Thompson who would eventually be the company's Operations Director joined the company in 1961; his first job was delivering parts on the company push bike. Bob soon progressed in the company, moving first into the warehouse then to counter sales and later to branch management and taking special responsibility for the company's exhaust business. In time almost 30 warehouses would be reporting to Bob as well as four regional operational managers.

Another early stalwart was Roy Naylor, who would become the company's Purchasing Director; he joined the business in 1965 as a young man in the stores and, like Bob Thompson, moved on the counter sales and later to branch management. Today he has a team reporting to him and has responsibility for new products, stock development and looking after £11 million worth of stock, all controlled centrally from the head office.

*Left and below: Examples of the first hydraulic jacks and lifts imported from the USA.*

In 1967 a major rebuilding project took place at Mabgate when some of the property was demolished and a three storey building, Apson House, erected in its place at a cost of £50,000 giving around 15,000 sq ft of floor space. Service Equipment (Leeds) now joined its parent at Mabgate. New premises were also built for the Wakefield branch in the same year.

Jim Page's son, Andrew Page, joined the company in 1974 after completing a business course in Leeds and working in Germany for a year and a half where he worked for Robert Bosch GmbH in Stuttgart and with a Bosch distributor in Celle near Hanover.

By 1977, coincidentally the year the company took delivery of its first computer, annual sales had reached a million pounds. By 1980 sales were over two million pounds and company auditors had recommended reconstituting the company to permit a partitioning of the Page and Purchon family's shareholdings in the company and its subsidiaries. In the process the company name was changed to simply Andrew Page Ltd, its new board of directors being Jim Page, the Chairman and Managing Director, Andrew Page, HM Gorman and Joan Page. Sadly HM Gorman suffered a heart attack the following year and although it would not be until 1986 that he passed away he would never fully recover.

The year of HM Gorman's heart attack, after his 25 years with the company, was also tragically marked by the death of Joan Page. However, despite these personal worries for the directors, sales continued to soar, exceeding £3 million in 1982 with a new Bradford depot opening later in the year.

Yet another depot was opened in York in 1984, a year in which sales again increased, to record levels of over £4 million. Such growth created problems of its own in simply keeping track of the business. In 1987, having decided to increase the financial and accounting skills within the company, its accountant's

***Top:*** *Andrew Page & Son Limited celebrating the Coronation.* ***Above:*** *James Page, founder of today's Andrew Page Ltd.*

recruitment service was asked to advertise in order to recruit a Finance Director. Recruitment consultants Binder Hamlyn began interviewing that July and presented the directors with four candidates for their final choice; as a result Martin G Ingham was invited to join the company that August and would subsequently become Financial Director. Meanwhile during the earlier months of the year considerable time had been spent in examining sites in Lancashire as possible locations for the firm's first branch over on the other side of the Pennines. That June a site had been identified in Bury and negotiations for the property had commenced, though it would not be until March of the following year that the branch on Bury's Bridge Trading estate would actually open.

Once again sales increased, sales for the year end 31st May 1989 would be £8.2 million whilst in November of that year the company's 169 staff achieved a record breaking £1.14 worth of sales in a single month.

In March 1990 staff were saddened to hear of the death of Ken Purchon. Though Ken had resigned his directorship in 1980 his friendship and advice had always been highly valued by the company.

In April 1990 the company accepted an offer of £106,500 for its freehold premises in Wakefield and immediately took out a lease for larger premises in Grantley Way, Wakefield. That same month Andrew Page visited M&R Components Ltd in Washington, Tyne and Wear to meet its directors and as a result that complete business was acquired for £220,000.

Nor would that acquisition be the only growth in 1990. That June a lease for a second branch west of the Pennines was signed leading to a warehouse being opened in Stockport the following November.

The next year the company was able to buy the freehold of its headquarters at Apson House in Mabgate for £385,000. As a result major works were now put in place. The battery store at 59 Mabgate was refurbished as was

*Top*: *A company outing to Dagenite Battery Factory in 1949.* *Left*: *The Wakefield sales counter in 1969.* *Below*: *Andrew Page and Son's premises in Mabgate in 1961.*

company he had founded so long ago was now the largest independently owned motor factor in the country. By 1997 the company's turnover had reached more than £30 million and was employing some 400 staff and utilising 52 cars and 149 vans.

Andrew Page's daughter Victoria, the fourth generation of the Page family, joined the company in 1999 working for the Operations Director on the employment and recruitment side of the business.

Today 95 per cent of the business is within the UK, supplying independent repair garages, independent and national fast fit exhaust and repair outlets, main dealers, local council workshops and specialist diesel workshops.

the first floor of Apson House. When completed that floor would accommodate the firm's complete office operation together with its computer section and buying office, whilst a larger car park was created for staff and clients.

By now sales had increased yet again: the £10 million mark had been passed in 1991 and now, with over 200 staff, annual sales had reached a staggering £13 million: this despite the severe recession which had been affecting trade and the economy over the previous two years. The recession was said to be the deepest and longest since the second world war and economists forecast that the downturn would last until 1994: in fact the following year Andrew Page Ltd would notch up sales of almost £18 million!

On 2nd November 1992 Jim Page relinquished his role as Managing Director and handed over that baton to his son Andrew, though he continued as company Chairman. The following week the company's ninth branch opened; this was at Thirsk in North Yorkshire and would be an experimental branch operating as a satellite of the Harrogate branch from which it received its supplies and was intended to service a geographical area beyond the economic service ability of its parent branch. A second satellite branch would open in Bramley the following March whilst an eleventh branch would open in Huddersfield in March 1994, helping push annual sales over the £20 million mark. The following years would be characterised by the opening of branch after branch across the whole of the North of England. In June 1996, the company's fiftieth anniversary, Jim Page was able to read in 'Motor Trader ' magazine an article reporting that the

The company has become known for keeping top quality products from the same manufacturers and is famed for the reliability and speed of its deliveries.

After the war, when the company began, the range of products carried was small with few vehicles on the road. Customers would philosophically wait for their parts, and in many cases would also stockpile parts in their own workshops. Today the company stocks over 70,000 different parts covering some 150 manufacturers. The company needs to keep most parts in stock as today customers demand instant service. The customer need make a call only when the vehicle is stripped down

***Top left:*** *The company's Leeds branch, in the early 1970s.* ***Above right and right****: An interior view of the well stocked Andrew Page warehouse and sales counter.*

company keeps up with the technical developments, the company has appointed a technical manager to keep up with improvements made by the car manufacturers. Meanwhile the company is aiming to continue to grow in the north of England and intends to eventually have a branch/warehouse in every major town and city up to the Scottish border whilst continuing to maintain the family feeling that the business still prides itself on.

In the opening years of the 21st century the company is financially very strong; this has been achieved by ploughing back cash continuously into the business, making the company financially independent; it also means that it can expand at whatever rate it feels comfortable with. The company now has around 700 full time employees and a number of part timers as well - a long way from its original two. The majority of staff have been with the company for many years; this means that its customers get to know them well and that the company's skills in understanding and sometimes interpreting their needs and requests is unsurpassed.

Sadly, on September 30th 2001, the Chairman and founder of Andrew Page Ltd, James Readdie Page, died at his home, just before his 84th birthday.

Despite the loss of its founder the company's work still goes on under Andrew Page. In 2002 the 30th site opened in Sunderland. Annual sales now exceed £50 million, an extraordinary example of how business acumen and hard work can, over the course of a working life, turn an investment of just a few hundred pounds into one of the regions most prominent companies.

and ready for repair. This means the Andrew Page delivery service has to be hourly to most customers, and in some cases half -hourly.

The company takes understandable pride in its delivery service. In contrast with its bicycle delivery days the firm now has over 350 delivery vans running around the branches and covers most of the north of England. Around 165,000 deliveries are made each month, of which an astonishing 120,000 are made within sixty minutes of an order being received.

All Andrew Page warehouses carry a very full range of parts, whilst half a dozen carry almost every part the company supplies. There is no central warehouse since the firm believes that it must have parts availability as near to its customers as possible.

Inevitably the company is highly computerised and could not handle the volumes and speed of business without being so. The firm's own computer department develops its ever more sophisticated computer systems in-house.

In recent years the parts sold have become increasingly expensive and much more technically advanced, and this is expected to continue. In response, to make sure the

***Top left and above left***: *Part of the Andrew Page fleet.*
***Below***: *Managing Director, Andrew Page.*

# Wartime

**Below:** It is a wet day and the war is on. What is there to smile about? It is the end of a working day and there is even a queue for the trams. All we need now is for the air raid siren to sound and we shall all have to run for the air-raid shelters in City Square. The steps up to the shelter, and the corners of the doors, have been painted white so that the door can be found in the darkness during a 'blackout'. If the enemy can just wait until we get home there is the Anderson shelter in the garden. Granddad erected it and dug the hole for it to rest in. He covered it with soil and a few sand bags. Mother planted some flowers over it. We don't like to admit that she found a bit of old carpet from somewhere and put it inside. 'We could be here a long time before the all-clear sounds', she said. It was better than the Morrison shelter our neighbours had. That was a strong metal cage, into which they climbed when the siren sounded. It was capable of holding up the rubble should the house take a direct hit. All they had to do then was await rescue. Many people made a sheet of plywood to cover it, and hid it with a tablecloth. Decorated with a vase of flowers, or a plaster statue of a lady holding the lead of an energetic dog, it was transformed into a piece of useful furniture.

The posters, on the outer walls of the recruitment office shelter, encourage young ladies to join the Land Army, and don the familiar khaki green or brown uniform.

It was 'Salute the Soldier' in 1944, and well they might salute him, for the war was at a critical turning point and every penny would help to bring it to a swift conclusion. The National Savings Campaign target was six million pounds, which was the sum needed to send one hundred divisions to Berlin. The crowd stood attentive to every word uttered by the Chancellor of the Exchequer, Sir John Anderson. Every eye was on him. Then the people of Leeds went away and worked and generously gave £1,614,658 in the first few days. This at a time when the average wage for a family was about £8. The people were accustomed to the themes for collecting. With an aim in view, and a target to achieve, they willingly worked and gave. Sometimes it would be to 'Buy a Spitfire', and other times a warship of some kind. They gave their aluminium pans when there was a scare that the aeroplane manufacturers would run out of supplies of the metal. They would have been upset if they knew that many of the pots and pans collected were never used. Some folks returned home, possibly from the cinema where they may have seen Humphrey Bogart in the popular film 'Casablanca', or Noel Coward in the film 'In Which We Serve', only to discover that the railings had been taken from outside their houses and churches to make bombs, bullets, and guns. The town hall steps have been painted with white squares to help in the dark nights of blackout. Better to trip on a step than to help an enemy bomber by showing a light. By the end of the 'Salute the Soldier' campaign, the people of Leeds had raised a staggering £6,848,594!

**Above:** A shot down German plane is the centre of attention in the city. One less for the people of Leeds to worry about. The line of sandbags surround the edge of City Square and by this time the Second World War was at its fiercest. Leeds had a share of the bombing by the Luftwaffe. The Museum and the Town Hall were damaged and Wellington Street, which had a railway and a goods yard, was a major target. Quarry Hill flats which also had a goods yard in front of it was hit and a gas main was severed. St Peter's church suffered a direct hit but no one was injured. Generally, Leeds however was very fortunate compared to other industrial cities.

One of the most interesting stories about the city's role in the war involved Waddingtons, the game manufacturers. The firm produced maps painted on silk cloths for prisoners of war and servicemen lost behind enemy lines. Waddingtons also produced Monopoly boards containing hidden maps and currency. It is estimated that half of the British prisoners who escaped used a Waddingtons map. By 1944 thirty thousand of these maps were being made each week. That is a fascinating story, yet however much it may sound incredible, the more that we think about it the easier it is to comprehend the logicality of it all. Crises do bring out the most innovative solutions and usually inventions and developments are the result of having to deal with a difficulty or a desperate need. So Waddingtons came up trumps!

**Top right:** Under the watchful eye of the local constable, these members of the armed forces cross to climb aboard the tram for Roundhay Park. They are relaxed and fully at ease. Wearing non-regulation shoes, and with their hair plastered in place with hair cream, they fear no charge for being improperly dressed. Those who have decided to wear headgear have placed it at a rakish tilt so as not to damage the wavy creation. They have earned the right for it is now June 1945 and the hard fought victory is with us.

The conductor is curious to know why the cameraman is bothering to record such a mundane scene. He does not realise that he is to become a part of an historical record. They do not mind posing for the camera, for to be caught

# Events of the 1940s

### MELODY MAKERS
The songs of radio personalities such as Bing Crosby and Vera Lynn were whistled, sung and hummed everywhere during the 1940s. The 'forces' sweetheart' brought hope to war-torn Britain with 'When the Lights go on Again', while the popular crooner's 'White Christmas' is still played around Christmas time even today. Who can forget songs like 'People Will Say we're in Love', 'Don't Fence Me In', 'Zip-a-dee-doo-dah', and 'Riders in the Sky'?

### INVENTION AND TECHNOLOGY
Inspired by quick-drying printers' ink, in 1945 Hungarian journalist Laszlo Biro developed a ballpoint pen which released viscous ink from its own reservoir as the writer moved the pen across the page. An American inventor was working on a similar idea at the same time, but it was Biro's name that stuck. A few years later Baron Bich developed a low cost version of the pen, and the 'Bic' ballpoint went on sale in France in 1953.

### SCIENCE AND DISCOVERY
In 1943 Ukrainian-born biochemist Selman Abraham Waksman made a significant discovery. While studying organisms found in soil he discovered an antibiotic (a name Waksman himself coined) which was later found to be the very first effective treatment for tuberculosis. A major killer for thousands of years, even the writings of the ancient Egyptians contain stories of people suffering from tuberculosis. Waksman's development of streptomycin brought him the 1952 Nobel Prize for Medicine.

on film is better than the experience of being caught by the enemy. When the tram arrives in the Park, there will be many hundreds more, ten thousand in fact, who, like them, had been prisoners of war. The reunion was organised by the Yorkshire Evening News to say thank you to them on behalf of a grateful nation. When they are eventually demobilised, or 'demobbed', and they return to normal work in 'Civvy Street', they will receive a clothing coupon, which they will then be able to spend at the Fifty Shilling Tailors. Montague Burton's tailoring shop offered a full three-piece suit for fifty shillings (two pounds and fifty pence). The jacket, waistcoat and trousers were called 'the full Monty'. How has that expression changed to mean what it means today we wonder?

They turned out in hundreds to watch their brave sons march by. It was the Ark Royal Week parade on 6th May 1942. The city had 'adopted' the aircraft carrier in November 1941, but she was sunk during a battle in the Mediterranean Sea. As they passed the town hall steps no lesser person than General De Gaulle of the Free French Forces took the salute. It was part of the War Savings Week in 1942 and the City of Leeds had set itself the target of £5,000,000, but the hard working and generous people of Leeds almost doubled that figure. They raised over £9,000,000. Whilst the crowd had turned out to show their admiration for the men and women in the armed forces, one cannot help admiring the members of the crowd too, for they had made great sacrifices. As we look closely at them, as they stand in the square, we cannot help but notice that they are smartly attired. Despite rationing, they have spent their clothing coupons wisely. They have revamped their old clothes, as they were encouraged to do on film, radio and in government organised exhibitions. Many houses owned a cobbler's last, so that a cheap repair could be made to leaking shoes. As granny used to say, 'It costs nowt to wash and make sure your shoes are clean', and, 'You're not properly dressed without your hat'. It was unthinkable to venture into town without looking your best. 'We may be poor, but we have our pride', she always added.

**Above:** The Headrow in 1942 paints a very sombre and bleak picture. It is the third year of the war and emergency procedures are well in force. Military personnel appear to outnumber civilians. Lamp standards carry no bulbs because of black out regulations and huge civil defence water tanks are sited in front of Lewis's Department store in case of bomb attacks from the air. In front of the store itself there are large brick bomb blast barriers to protect those inside should there be an air raid. A very bleak outlook! It is hard to imagine anything worthwhile coming out of this state of affairs. However what was one consolation was to change for the time being, at least, the role and status of women. Popular images like 'Rosie the Riveter' were used to recruit women to fill defence jobs which suffered from the shortage of men. Women were transformed into shipbuilders, welders, riveters and machine workers. Leeds, playing a vital part in industrial and military production, was well to the forefront in this scheme. But at the end of the war the inevitable happened. New propaganda was produced which encouraged women to leave the workforce so that men could resume their old jobs. It was estimated that 80 per cent of the female workforce wanted to keep their skilled jobs but they were laid off in great numbers. So 'Rosie the Riveter' returned home to be 'Rosie the Meat Roaster'.

# On the move

**Below:** The date is not known, when the camera shutter fell to capture this scene of tram number 137 leaving the square on route 27. Route 27 ran to Cardigan Road and dropped passengers at the County Cricket ground. It could be that it was in the late 40s or early 50s as lampposts still sported the black and white stripes much needed in the days of the blackout, although the car has none of the required louvered covers on its headlamps. Even in the 50s there were many reminders of the war. Ration books stayed with us until May 1950. There was an outcry when the grand, ornate, Standard Life Assurance building, seen on the right of the picture, was demolished and replaced by an austere, modern, sixties style building. It was not long before that too was demolished and replaced by the Norwich Union building that is there today. The Post Office building remains as it was here, except that it was cleaned, like many others, after the Clean-Air Act came into effect in the late 50s. How strange, to our modern eye, the spiders web of wires above, and the pattern of tramlines below, now seem. Built between 1925 and 1928, there were two hundred of these 'Chamberlain' trams in service. They were the largest single type of tram in Leeds. The last of these ran in 1957, and the last of any kind in 1959.

Prams were not so portable in 1954, but they were beautifully made and could carry a few bags of shopping too without making the baby uncomfortable or making it unstable. Their disadvantages didn't show quite so much when tolerant drivers were willing to keep the 247 on number 11 route to Gipton Estate waiting until pram and mother were safely aboard. The man on the pavement looks ready to lend a hand should one be needed. Why is it that there seemed to be more time for things in those days? One man, who certainly seemed to be in a hurry this year, was a young 25 year-old man called Roger Bannister. He ran so fast that he broke the four-minute barrier for the mile at Oxford on the 6th May. The Inspector seems to be keeping shoppers in an orderly queue outside Dewhurst's. Could it be Blakey from 'On the buses'? The ladies have a lot to talk about because the newspapers were announcing that, from July onwards, ration books could be thrown away. Although sweets had not been rationed for a year people seemed to have got used to being without sugary things, and were eating less of them than they did before the war. The stalls in Kirkgate market were now better stocked and luxury items were steadily returning to the shops. It was in this market that Michael Marks began with just one stall. When he went into partnership with Mr Spencer an empire grew.

# Events of the 1960s

### HOT OFF THE PRESS

*Barbed wire, concrete blocks and a wide no-man's-land divided East from West when a reinforced wall was built right across the city of Berlin in 1961. Many East Germans escaped to the West at the eleventh hour, taking with them only the possessions they could carry. The Berlin Wall divided the city - and hundreds of family members and friends - for 28 years until the collapse of Communist rule across Eastern Europe. Who can ever forget those scenes in 1989, when ordinary people themselves began to physically tear down the hated wall?*

### THE WORLD AT LARGE

*'One giant leap for mankind' was taken on 20th July 1969, when Neil Armstrong made history as the first man to set foot on the moon. During the mission he and fellow-astronaut 'Buzz' Aldrin collected rock and soil samples, conducted scientific experiments - and had a lot of fun jumping around in the one-sixth gravity. Twenty-one hours and thirty-seven minutes after their landing they took off again in their lunar module 'Eagle' to rejoin Apollo II which was orbiting above them, proudly leaving the American flag on the Moon's surface.*

### ROYAL WATCH

*Princess Margaret's announcement in 1960 that she was to wed photographer Antony Armstrong-Jones (later Lord Snowdon) brought sighs of relief from her immediate family. Just five years earlier the people of Britain had sympathised as the princess bowed to public and private pressure, ending her relationship with Peter Townsend, Prince Philip's former equerry. The Church (and the Queen, as its Head) frowned on the liaison as Townsend was divorced. Her marriage to Lord Snowdon itself ended in 1978.*

As work is going on next door to Dolcis, now the premises of the Alliance and Leicester, tram number 120 passes on route 2, the Moortown Circular. We are not sure the time of day, as the tram hides the square clock hanging outside H Samuel's shop, but the milkman is still busy with deliveries so perhaps we can assume it is still early morning. We are given a choice - we can either have one of Orme's boiled sweets, or drink Tizer 'appetizer' (both advertised on the tram), or we can quench our thirst with a bottle of milk from the passing milkman. Milk was always considered good for the health, so much so that the government decided that it should be given to all children in school. Some dreaded playtime because they did not like it, and that was when a child could discover who their friends were, as they had to take an empty bottle back to the milk crate under the watchful eye of the teacher. The tram is a 'Chamberlain' or 'Pivotal' car. There were two hundred of them in total and the last one was taken from service in 1957. Just visible to the right of the door is a cord that is fastened to the bow collector. When the car reached the end of the line the conductor would swing on the cord with his full weight to pull the collector over. There was just enough slackness in the overhead wire to allow the collector to pivot and face the opposite direction. Meanwhile the driver disconnected the brass steering and brake handles and moved to the opposite end to begin the return journey.

As the traffic rumbles over the cobblestones on Leeds Bridge heading for Briggate, they have to move aside for the tram. The tram cannot side step, nor can it leave the track unless, if we believe the poster, the conductor, having drunk some Guinness, could lift it out of the way. There is no need to worry, however, for, at the end of a strenuous day of pulling your horse inside the cart, or moving the tram, you can be sure of a good night's sleep if you drink your Bourn-Vita. It was possible to buy a mug with a face, just like the one on the poster but minus the sleeping cap. Perhaps, if there are any in existence today, they are now 'collectable'. The Golden Lion, which can be seen in the background, was once one of the many coaching houses in Leeds. The journey, from Leeds to London, took between three and four days and cost two pounds eight shillings. A shilling, for those who do not remember a time before decimalisation, was the equivalent of five new pence. The Old George, on the opposite side of the road, is reputedly the George Inn mentioned in Jane Eyre. The whole of Briggate is rich with such historical Inns tucked away in alleys and corners. Not far up the road from our photographer in an alley in Duncan Street is The Whip. It is said to have sold more beer, in the years between the wars, than any other pub. It also had the reputation of catering for men only.

**Above:** There were 938 dwellings on Quarry Hill housing 2500 people mostly in 2,3 and 4 bedroomed coal fired flats. It was obvious that to cater for the needs of the area and for the city's expanding population a new transport amenity was required. So in 1938 so close by the estate and adjacent to the markets area a new bus station was opened at a cost of £44000. Ominously it contained an air raid shelter, which would accommodate a mere 150 people. War was just around the corner and no matter how hard people had hoped and prayed it would never happen, there was certain inevitability about it, unfortunately. It hung like a dark cloud above the world. When it did come, it had it affected new Quarry Hill in two ways. One was the need to have erected air raid shelters in the open spaces and secondly the recreation ground that was to contain bowling greens and tennis courts was never completed. In fact during that period it suffered from a great deal of neglect, so much so it became an eyesore. After the war, however, tenant agitation proved valuable and soon these amenities so crucial in the scheme were provided. Quarry Hill could now prosper, although the war years, which hopefully would have seen the dreams of the designers for a totally community based estate, had torn a hole in their plans. It was now up to the residents to fulfil the dream.

The Aire and Calder Navigation canal was built through the vision of nine gentlemen from Leeds, and nine from Wakefield. They formed a company to build a waterway to link the city with the sea. Like these men of old, the people of Leeds have had the vision to build new, whilst preserving the old and the good. The Giotto tower, inspired by the Giotto bell tower in Florence, and the Verona tower, from the design of the Lambeth Tower in Verona, can be seen rising up beyond the Leeds and Liverpool canal office. There was no expense spared, when these towers were constructed, to hide the chimneys of Harding and Son's busy mills. They give charm and interest as much today as they did when they were first conceived. Carrying goods on packhorse over inadequate roads would no longer be enough to satisfy the demands of the industries in Leeds and the surrounding districts. Those who designed and built the canals could not possibly have imagined the developments of the present day. They would have been amused by the idea that there could be a tourist industry around their waterways, or that their warehouses may one day become 'desirable residencies'. Perhaps, if the traffic grinds to a halt along the M62, their canals may find interest from industry once more. When they were first cut, the locks were planned with a minimum width of fourteen feet and two inches to accommodate the barges of the time. At the height of their use they linked the East Coast to the West and could, on the main channels, carry barges that were one hundred and twenty feet long, with a width of seventeen and a half feet. How many of us have sat on the canal bank, optimistically dangling a worm impaled on a bent pin, in the hopes of catching a giant fish? Granny tied a piece of string around the neck of a jam jar for us to carry the stickleback catch of the day back home.

**Below:** In the 40s black and white stripes became very fashionable. They were a necessary decoration during the blackout. There were no streetlights after dark. The cowled headlamps of cars, buses, and other vehicles, shed little light, and the stripes did help to prevent some collisions. They were put on the edge of the pavement, as here at stand B in Central Bus Station Eastgate, to help pedestrians and drivers to see the kerb edge. They were painted around lampposts and telegraph poles, just as they have been on the rails here at the bus stop. Like the army saying, 'If it doesn't move - paint it! If it does move - salute it!' At night there were strict blackout laws. Times for blackout were announced on the wireless, and a Warden came around regularly to check. Any chink of light could mean prosecution and a fine. Many homes hung a blanket across the door on the inside so that no light showed as the door was opened. No good giving the enemy bombers a target to aim for.

On such a murky day as this in November 1943, when St Peter's church can only just be seen from the bus station, there was less danger of enemy bombs being accurately targeted. On a clear night, with a full moon, a 'bomber's moon', the rivers and canals shone clearly. Even the polished railway and tramlines could be seen. They drew a map for any enemy aircraft flying over. Leeds did receive a few enemy bombs, but the city was a little more fortunate than many other parts of the country.

**Below right:** Passengers for Cottingley travel up North Street in the number eight Daimler bus past the junction with New York Road. It is a lovely day in 1965 and the gentlemen can venture forth without an overcoat. Even the most conservative men were now wearing coloured shirts and flowery ties. The Beatles made Italian style suits popular. The Beatles, who one major recording company rejected because they felt that they were not good enough to make it to the top, had by this date had eleven number one singles. Another 'chart topper' was the Morris Minor, an example of which is parked by the kerb. The millionth car had rolled off the production line in 1961. Alexander Issigonis, who had designed the revolutionary 'mini' in 1959, designed the Minor as far back as 1948. In 1948 it had cost £280 new, but by 1961 it had reached £416. The single storey shops on the left of the picture were built in the gardens of the Bischoff family home, also known as Sheepscar Hall. It was once a beautiful eighteenth century house and was owned by Nathaniel Denison in 1725. It was demolished to make way for the inner ring road. But, whilst many historically interesting buildings have been lost in the name of progress, Leeds still holds many architectural gems.

**Bottom:** The year is 1968 and, with increasing prosperity, more people could afford to own a car. At the beginning of the sixties, only one in 24 had enough money to buy a car of their own. Now, with a stronger economy and stable employment, the figure was one in seven. Washing the car became a regular Sunday morning pastime when they were polished and waxed. The constantly increasing volume of traffic was a national problem, and the government appointed Colin Buchanan to prepare a report. Long before that report appeared, the City of Leeds was planning an inner ring road to deflect traffic away from the congested centre. It had been proposed as early as 1951. It was a daring plan that needed ruthless determination as it carved its' way through the city. Such plans cannot come too soon for these frustrated motorists. When they do eventually reach the centre, they will be greeted by problems in parking. Meters had been introduced three years earlier and they charged sixpence (2.5p) per hour, and fixed penalty fines were also operating. Oh the joys of motoring!

These are the days before Leeds City Transport amalgamated with those of Huddersfield, Halifax and Bradford. For the enthusiast, the number six, plying its' way to the corn exchange, is an AEC Regent V Metro Cammell Orion 914. It is passing buildings, which in 1965 had not yet been swept away by the bulldozer. Behind it can be seen the Midland Bank standing at Golden Cross junction, giving us a clue as to where these buildings once stood. Fares were collected by a conductor, or conductress, who kept schoolboys in order, and prevented them, whenever possible, from hanging from the rear platform and dropping in a run before the bus had come to a stop. The driver received one ring of the bell to stop and two to go, and wasn't there trouble if little boys rang it for 'fun'? On the first day in 1965, continental road signs were adopted, as recommended by the Warboy's Committee. Mandatory instructions to be enclosed in a red circle, advisory signs in a rectangle, and informational signs became triangular in shape. The traditional 'Halt' sign at major roads was changed for a 'more easily understood' sign that simply said 'Stop'. The comedians of the time may great fun of the changes at the time, and remarks were made about the continentals dictating, and loss of 'national identity'. Sounds familiar doesn't it? Cars, like the Hillman Imp, which is passing the bus, and the Austin following, now had to be fitted with flashing indicators and brake stoplights. Gone were the eccentric and temperamental orange indicator arms, which lifted from their slot in the doorpost, or not as was often the case on a winter's morning.

# *Shopping spree*

**Below:** In this 1965 photograph of Boar Lane everything appears tranquil enough. No need for panic and rush as this lady tries to cross the road. The Morris Minor poses no threat. This model was introduced in 1948 and among enthusiasts still retains its popularity almost to the extent it has a cult following. Car parking does not seem a problem either. There is here a mixture of the old and new and with hindsight a portent of things to come. The striped pole of Jackson's barbers shop under the Griffin Hotel represents the old among others. The Griffin, which takes its name from a mythical monster fabled to be an offspring of a lion and an eagle, was originally a coaching inn. In the background in City Square is the famous Majestic, which opened as a cinema in 1922 on the site of a Temperance Hotel. It suited its name with its wide spacious auditorium and possessed its own Symphony orchestra and magnificent organ. It was only 4 years after this photograph that it closed as a cinema. Thankfully it is a listed building so its grandeur can still be appreciated. The new is represented by the growth of chain stores and office blocks such as the Provincial Insurance building, the likes of which are so much a feature of modern city life. How a city copes with the new developments without tearing out its own heart is a sign of careful planning. Looking at this photograph it is clear that Leeds has in this part of the city at least retained its shape and preserving as best it can what is worthwhile.

The date, when the camera clicked and captured this sunny picture of Commercial Street, is not certain. It is possible that it is just before war broke out. If this is the case, then for these shoppers rationing may yet be a horrid possibility. Should any of them faint at the thought of such a thing they can now dial an emergency telephone number. The 999 call was introduced in 1937, partly in response to a typhoid epidemic that hit the country in that year, to get speedy assistance. The public telephones could be operated by inserting two pence, and dialling a simple number. It was fatal to press button 'A' until there was an answer at the other end of the line, because your money would be heard dropping into the box to be lost forever. If button 'B' was pressed, when there was no reply, your money was returned. A penny was of some value then and after the war - three could get a child into the Tower Picture House on a Saturday afternoon, and one could provide the ride on the tram to get there, or buy an ice cream at the interval. The builders, maintaining the buildings in Commercial Street, could not have guessed that one day one of the shops would be selling items resulting from an empire begun by Walt Disney the creator of Mickey Mouse. All of the cars in the street are built on a chassis. They have no power steering, and, in many cases, no form of heater either. A travelling rug stretched across the knees of a passenger was an essential item. Direction was indicated to other road users by an arm through an open window, or by those orange indicator arms, which had a tendency to stay in their mounting on a cold day.

# Events of the 1940s

### HOT OFF THE PRESS
*At the end of World War II in 1945 the Allies had their first sight of the unspeakable horrors of the Nazi extermination camps they had only heard of until then. In January, 4,000 emaciated prisoners more dead than alive were liberated by the Russians from Auschwitz in Poland, where three million people, most of them Jews, were murdered. The following year 23 prominent Nazis faced justice at Nuremberg; 12 of them were sentenced to death for crimes against humanity.*

### THE WORLD AT LARGE
*The desert area of Alamogordo in New Mexico was the scene of the first atomic bomb detonation on July 16, 1945. With an explosive power equal to more than 15,000 tons of TNT, the flash could be seen 180 miles away.*
*President Truman judged that the bomb could secure victory over Japan with far less loss of US lives than a conventional invasion, and on 6th August the first of the new weapons was dropped on Hiroshima. Around 80,000 people died.*

### ROYAL WATCH
*By the end of World War II, the 19-year-old Princess Elizabeth and her distant cousin Lieutenant Philip Mountbatten RN were already in love. The King and Queen approved of Elizabeth's choice of husband, though they realised that she was rather young and had not mixed with many other young men. The engagement announcement was postponed until the Princess had spent four months on tour in Africa. The couple's wedding on 20th November 1947 was a glittering occasion - the first royal pageantry since before the war.*

**Left:** There are few shoppers in Boar Lane on this day in 1946, and the one we can plainly see has little in her basket. Goods are slowly returning to the shops, but the ration book is still needed. The government of the time had warned that things would get worse before they improved, and they did. Small children were being introduced to the wonders of the banana, and the method of peeling back the skin to reveal the hidden fruit. They were shown how to pick the seeds of the pomegranate with a pin. Adults were surprised to discover that their offspring did not enjoy these 'treats'. They were tastes that many of them never did quite manage to acquire. Quite what this lady made of the newly introduced two-piece bathing costume that had been designed this year we can only guess. Its inventor named it after some islands in the Pacific Ocean. He called it the Bikini. Perhaps he chose the name before the Americans exploded the atomic bomb underwater near the islands, or was he aware that it too would cause a minor explosion when it was presented to the public? There was a clacking of tongues. It was called 'rude' and 'disgusting' it was clear that it would undermine the structure of our entire society. It was 'itsy bitsy teeny weeny', in yellow polka dots, and sung about. The girl wearing it, we are told in the song, 'was afraid to come out of the water'. She could have, in the opinion of many of the time, spent her hard earned money, and valuable coupons, better if she had bought warm utility underwear!

**Above:** The tram lines are very much in evidence in this 1955 photograph of the junction of Boar Lane and Briggate as we look towards the Corn Exchange. The shops give us reminders of the past with names we do not see today. Think of Home and Colonial. It reminds us of Maypole, Liptons and Broughs. They actually all became part of the Home and Colonial group, although they did continue to trade under their original names. The stateliness of the buildings is very much in the fashion of Boar Lane and, of course the jewel, is the Corn Exchange. Motorists generally tend not to see that building these days as they negotiate the intricacies of the traffic system but the building itself is a marvel. It appears circular but is in fact elliptical on an area barely equivalent to fifty-four square yards. The dome is seventy-five feet high at its highest point. Glazed roof panels were designed to ensure that light reached all areas and a colonnaded balcony gave access to the many small offices. It is a triumph to Victorian engineering. Originally it was the centre of a thriving corn trade and now refurbishment has allowed it to play a more contemporary role in the city's commercial life. The sedateness of the area we see here compares to the hustle and bustle of today and even more so with earlier times. At the bottom of Briggate in the seventeenth century a fair was held twice weekly attracting visitors from far afield. Stalls ranged in all directions even as far as the bridge over the Aire. Congestion is not a modern problem, obviously.

The shop which is receiving a facelift in this 1955 photograph dates back to 1613, evidence indeed of Briggate's long standing commercial importance. This importance to the city's life is still very much in evidence today as we note the names and styles of the establishments which have replace those pictured here. Making it a pedestrianised area has been a benefit. As we see in the photograph the tramlines are still here and there is none of the congestion which this part of the city can expect later. The competition for road space was about to begin and it would not be long before they had been completely phased out. But everything goes round in circles. Who would bet against their reintroduction on a large scale?

Further up on the opposite side of the road from the Pack Horse stands the then famous Empire theatre, host to many if not all the music hall stars. Frank Matcham, architect of many theatres, including the Keighley Queens Theatre and Opera House, later known as the Hippodrome, designed the Empire. It was at the Empire that the great escapologist Harry Houdini failed to escape - from a barrel of Tetley's ale. And he was teetotal. Fortunately a fellow artist, who pulled him out half conscious, saved him. Mr Houdini did not realise that ale gives off carbon dioxide. The theatre is now the Empire Arcade having closed in February 1961 with a performance of 'Babes in the Wood'.

**Above:** Look at this 1965 photograph of Boar Lane and wonder not so much about here being so few vehicles and the absence of the hustle and bustle of today's pedestrian traffic but to such matters as what happened to Hays Ales? What was so exotic about Koh I Noor shop? What ever happened to Owen and Robinson? The coffee bar was a sign of the 1950s when they were all the rage with the trendsetters of the time. They seemed to arrive with Teddy Boys and the beginnings of rock 'n' roll. Think of Tommy Steele, 'discovered', it is said, singing in a coffee bar when cappuccino was a new rage. Recall Bill Haley and his Comets and his kiss curl! And juke boxes! Boar Lane is at the southern edge of the commercial centre of the city. It had been widened in the 1860s and developed as the most fashionable shopping area in Leeds, with the uniformity of style and height of its buildings, contrasting favourably with streets and roads close by. That dignity is still apparent here in this photograph. Today Boar lane is part of the city's transport box and certainly does not give one chance to stand and stare and appreciate and recall the grandeur of its past. There are still in many of its buildings, though not necessarily in their functions, reminders of how it would have looked over 40 years ago.

**Above:** It is the Co-operative Society building in Albion Street in March 1945. Comedians made jokes about the Co-op 'having branches everywhere', but it was no joke if you forgot mother's 'divvy' (dividend) number when you were sent on an errand to the local co-op. There seemed to be one close to everyone's home. The dividend gave mum that extra bit needed. Life was hard, and would continue to be so for a number of years after the end of the war. The shop windows would remain empty and those that did contain some stock were beyond the reach of many who had neither the money, nor the coupons, with which to buy the goods. Ladies continued to practice their knitting and sewing skills. Though the worst seemed to have passed, and victory seemed to be just around the corner, there were still plenty of reminders of the recent hardships. There is a cover over the radiator of one of the cars. The idea was to stop air from passing through the radiator until the engine had reached the optimum temperature, thus saving precious petrol. If the driver did not keep one eye on the temperature gauge, however, there was a possibility of overheating. One car has still not removed one cowl from its' headlamp. It is a souvenir of the blackout. Whilst regulations had not been officially lifted, there was little likelihood of prosecution.

**Right:** Of all the streets in Leeds one, which over the years has undergone the greatest transformation, is Briggate. It had been the city's main trading area since the thirteenth century when it was laid out as a planned street with thirty building plots on each side of this market street. This 1965 photograph is looking up Briggate into the heart of shopping land. It certainly prided itself on being the centre of the city's shopping life and justifiably still does. However it is the marvel of the arcades and inn yards that branch off from it, which give it its uniqueness and the restoration of these glass topped arcades, which is so fascinating. Their names have a distinctiveness and style. The Grand, completed in 1898 was built as a double arcade with 2 parallel banks of shops. It housed the Tower Cinema and an animated clock. The Queen's Arcade was described as 'architecturally elegant' when it was opened in 1889 and nothing has changed. Thornton's Arcade had as its great attraction for children of any age an animated clock depicting a scene from Scott's 'Ivanhoe'. Queen Victoria's diamond jubilee was commemorated with the Victoria Arcade. And the last to be built was to be the grandest of all - the County Arcade. These arcades centred round Briggate still enhance the area in terms of character compactness and style. To many they defeat shopping centres hands down.

# Events of the 1960s

WHAT'S ON?
Television comedy came into its own in the 1960s, and many of the shows that were favourites then went on to become classics. 'On the Buses', 'Steptoe and Son', 'Till Death Us Do Part' and 'The Army Game' kept audiences laughing, while the incredible talents of Morecambe and Wise, the wit of Des O'Connor - often the butt of the duo's jokes - and the antics of Benny Hill established them forever in the nation's affections.

GETTING AROUND
The 2nd March 1969 was a landmark in the history of aviation. The Anglo-French supersonic airliner Concorde took off for the first time from Toulouse in France. Concorde, which can cruise at almost twice the speed of sound, was designed to fly from London to New York in an incredible three hours twenty minutes. The event took place just weeks after the Boeing 747, which can carry 500 passengers to Concorde's modest 100, made its first flight.

SPORTING CHANCE
Wembley Stadium saw scenes of jubilation when on 30th July 1966 England beat West Germany 4-2 in the World Cup. The match, played in a mixture of sunshine and showers, had been a nailbiting experience for players and spectators alike from the very beginning when Germany scored only thirteen minutes into the game. It was Geoff Hurst's two dramatic goals scored in extra time that secured the victory and lifted the cup for England - at last.

# Making a living

ON SATURDAY
FEB. 4TH
from 11 a.m. to 5 p.m.

The Cars are here now
FOR SALE by PRIVATE TREATY
BEFORE AUCTION
step within

It would seem to be 'a lot of shout about nowt'. 'The finest chance you'll have this year'. There is, apparently, only one very unlikely looking customer observing from a cautionary distance. It seems to be a gateway to very little. But looks can be deceiving, for this is 'the little acorn that grew into the large oak'. It is Appleyard's on North Street, which had opened in the previous year, 1927. The company was founded by John Ernest Appleyard and quickly grew. Perhaps we are just too late for the auction and have missed the opportunity to buy a 1927 Morris. These were the days when a car stopped at a filling station like this one, and the driver remained in his seat to await the arrival of an attendant who would ask how much petrol was needed. Having delivered that amount to the tank, he would probably give the windscreen a quick wipe after checking the oil level in the engine. These were the halcyon days of motoring when one could expect an AA patrolman to deliver a smart salute as soon as he saw the chrome and yellow metal badge that was bolted to the bumper.

Speedometers had now become mandatory on cars, which seemed reasonable as some cars could now reach speeds of sixty miles per hour on a good straight road with a following wind. In 1927, white lines had been painted down the centre of the roads for the first time. Ladies could now vote at the age of twenty-one, the same as men - and some of them actually wanted to drive the car themselves (we are only joking ladies)!

# Events of the 1960s

*MELODY MAKERS*
*The 1960s: those were the days when the talented blues guitarist Jimi Hendrix shot to rock stardom, a youthful Cliff Richard charmed the nation with his 'Congratulations' and Sandie Shaw won the Eurovision Song Contest for Britain with 'Puppet on a String'. It was the combined musical talents of a group of outrageous working-class Liverpool lads, however, who formed the Beatles and took the world by storm with music that ranged from the experimental to ballads such as 'Yesterday'.*

*INVENTION AND TECHNOLOGY*
*A major step forward was made in 1960 when the laser was invented. An acronym for Light Amplification by Stimulated Emission of Radiation, the device produces a narrow beam of light that can travel for vast distances and is focused to give enormous power. Laser beams, as well as being able to carry far more information than radio waves, can also be used for surgery, cutting, drilling, welding and scores of other operations.*

*SCIENCE AND DISCOVERY*
*When the drug Thalidomide was first developed during the 1950s it was hailed as a wonder drug which would ease the distressing symptoms of pregnancy sickness. By the early 1960s the drug's terrible side effects were being discovered, when more than 3000 babies had been born with severe birth defects. Malformed limbs, defective eyes and faulty intestines were the heart-rending legacy left by Thalidomide.*

**Left:** A member of the Lupton family built this beautiful Tudor style terrace of shops. Alderman Charles Lupton was the chairman of the City Improvements Committee responsible for the widening of the Headrow in 1924. Mr Otty has placed his shed, and roll of cable, and what appears to be a temporary toilet, for his workmen who will soon commence the demolition of this architectural gem. The buildings are vacated. Soon the steel ball will be swung by a crane to shatter their mock Tudor walls. The lady in the picture cannot believe that they are to be sacrificed, in the name of progress. In the early sixties the Inner Ring Road carved its way through. Bold, and sometimes painful, decisions had to be taken, as traffic congestion grew worse by the day. These shops were known as 'Rothwell's Parade' after the prestigious furniture shop at the opposite end of the row from those shown in our picture. The store sold contemporary furniture of the time. The word 'contemporary' was commonly used as the name for the style of the sixties. There was a reaction to the 'utility' furniture of the fifties. Solid oiled teak dining tables and chairs were 'the in thing'. The machined surfaces of Swedish silver, and highly textured fabrics, attracted young couples setting up home. White was the fashionable colour for internal walls, and external doors and windows. The 'open plan' taste of the time created multi-purpose open spaces in houses of which many now had central heating.

**Above:** Back to back housing had been a feature of Leeds housing and Leeds had continued to build them right up to 1937. There was a programme however of slum clearance and this created what was the city's famous landmark the Quarry Hill flats, the biggest block of council flats in Europe. Any innovation in housing and one as revolutionary as this scheme would have a great impact especially as the planners appear to have realised that people needed to live their lives not just bound by the idea of 'work, eat, sleep'. This high rise, high density estate certainly was designed to meet the needs of the community for it had a shopping area, laundry, day nursery, play areas, open spaces, gardens and banks. There were lifts to all floors and a refuse disposal system from the kitchen of each flat to a central incinerator which itself provided heating for the central laundry. This amenity became an unofficial centre of political and social discussion and activity. Consider what the occupants had come from. Back to backs many of them, some in one up one down fifteen feet square cottages with sanitary conditions, primitive to say the least. Consider what replaced these slums as their inhabitants moved to Quarry Hill many of whom from what was at one time officially termed 'Quarry Hill Unhealthy Area'. A 1938 paradise indeed.

Between 1965 and 1970 the number of private cars in this country increased by 30 per cent and the number of all vehicles by 14 per cent. Cities like Leeds could not cope with the amount of traffic coming into and leaving the city centre. Lines of traffic navigating between other lines of parked cars became an everyday feature of city life. Local traffic and long distance were using the same roads. The population was moving out to the suburbs as new housing developments were being established; there was an urgent need for an effective transport system to serve it. Here the new inner ring road is being created and we can see the Quarry Hill Flats on the left. What this ring road did was to divert East/West traffic out of the city centre without creating a great diversion for it by creating an inner city motorway. This was an innovative way of tackling a serious and growing problem. It is said that as more roads are built so the volume of traffic increases. Consequently no lasting solution is ever found. Like the price of property, traffic problems are a popular topic of conversation and commuters and shoppers will all have tales to tell and complaints to make about subjects such as parking restrictions, traffic jams, hold ups and road works. That is the price road users have to pay sometimes.

# On the box

Yorkshire Television seems to have been with us forever. It was however only in early 1967 that 'our' television company acquired its five acre slum clearance site on Kirkstall Road from the city corporation.

Work began on building the new £4 million television studios in July 1967; they were officially opened in July 1968 by the Duchess of Kent watched over by luminaries such as YTV's first chairman Sir Richard Graham, Prime Minister Harold Wilson and Post Master General John Stonehouse.

The first programme after the Duchess of Kent had switched the transmitter on was from Headingley and featured the England v Australia test match. Though cricket may have filled much of that first day's output youngsters were not forgotten with a preview of a puppet series 'Jimmy Green and His Time Machine' and 'Sugarball' followed by 'Diane's Magic Book' which featured 12 year old Leslie Mewse, a pupil at Allerton High School, dressed in a Bo-Peep costume and reading fairy stories.

At 6.35 the first edition of 'Calendar' was broadcast, it featured a young Jonathan Aitken as a presenter. Calendar was followed by a new film, 'Mona McCluskey'. At 7.30 pm 'Coronation Street' should have followed - and it would have done so had it not been for a technicians' strike over the hills in Granadaland.

Building was not finished until July 1969; three months earlier the collapse of the giant 1,265 foot tall tubular steel mast at Emley Moor led many to fear that broadcasting in Yorkshire might prove short-lived. In fact 70 per cent coverage was restored within four days, whilst full coverage was restored in 27 days after a temporary, 680 foot, mast was erected. The present 1,080 concrete mast at Emley Moor was completed in 1971.

Today Yorkshire Television is part of Granada PLC and is one of the largest ITV companies serving a region of 6.5 million people and employing more than 1,000 staff. YTV produces over 1,000 hours of programming a year, programmes such as 'Heartbeat', 'Touch of Frost' - and the ever popular 'Emmerdale' which in 2002 celebrated 30 years on the air.

*Above:* Her Majesty the Queen outside the Woolpack. As part of her Golden Jubilee celebrational visit around the country the Queen visited the Emmerdale village in July 2002. **Below left:** Yorkshire Television's Calendar newsroom. **Below:** Cast from the highly popular 'Heartbeat'.

# *Stitches in time*

The invention of the sewing machine by American Walter Hunt USA in the 1830s would slowly revolutionise the world's garment industry.

A great many more changes have taken place in the garment making industry since the late Abraham Bellow, founder of the Bellow Machine Company, now based at Bellow House in Ellerby Lane, started his sewing machine business in Leeds just before the first world war. Originally trained as an engineer and sewing machine mechanic Abraham soon

*Above: An early company letterhead. Below: From left to right: Doreen Bellow (Lady Bellwin), Irwin Bellow (Lord Bellwin), Leah Bellow, Marshall Bellow, Abraham Bellow and Corinne Bellow.*

saw the possibilities inherent in supplying the needs of a growing local industry and resolved to be at the forefront of its development.

Abraham's early efforts were soon interrupted by the war and service in the Royal Flying Corps. It was only on his demobilisation in 1919 that he restarted his company with a capital of £100. That modest investment would one day lead not only to the creation of an internationally known business but also a peerage for one of Abraham's sons.

At first Abraham dealt in the reconditioning of sewing machines and supplying services to many small garment making firms in the Leeds area. His activities soon extended to the larger emerging firms such as Montague Burtons, Hepworths and Prices. It was early

*Leeds Telephones:*
*30221 & 2 (PTE. BCH. EX.)*
*Leeds Telegrams:*
*"BELLOW, LEEDS".*
*Code: BENTLEYS.*

*London Telephone:*
*BISHOPSGATE 7340.*
*London Telegrams:*
*"BELLOWMACH, BETH, LONDON".*
*Code: BENTLEYS.*

## BELLOW MACHINE COMPANY

INCORPORATING THE CENTRAL SEWING MACHINE CO.
SOLE PROPRIETOR: A. BELLOW, A.INST. R.I., M.INST. S.E.

### MACHINERY SPECIALISTS FOR THE CLOTHING & ALLIED TRADES

**LEEDS**
HEAD OFFICE
SHOWROOMS & WORKS
BELLOW HOUSE
GRAFTON STREET.
ALSO AT
77, NORTH STREET.

**LONDON**
OFFICES
AND SHOWROOMS
73, HIGH STREET
SHOREDITCH
E.I.

*The Largest Employers of Labour in Europe in this particular type of Business.*

in 1920 that the original firm, then called Central Sewing Machine Company, changed its name to the Bellow Machine Company Ltd and became a supplier of machinery and equipment not only to firms in the Leeds area but to many other garment manufactures throughout the country.

It was well known that in the early days Abraham Bellow thought nothing of giving machines to customers and telling them to pay for them when they could. Many of those customers would remain clients of the company for three generations or more, never forgetting the help they had been given in those far off days.

In 1925 Abraham Bellow decided to manufacture special purpose sewing machines, and over the following years various types were introduced into the Bellow range. As that manufacturing activity increased the demand for iron castings became greater and in 1936 a foundry was opened adjacent to the main factory in Grafton Street.

In those pre second world war years Abraham gathered around him an able team of engineers and sales people. By the 1960s and 70s there were many employees with well over 30 years service with the company. By the 1980s it was common for the sons of some of those early employees to hold high positions within the company.

From the 1920s onwards the founder, invariably accompanied by his wife Leah, whose own contribution

*Top: The Bellow Machine Company premises in 1968.*
*Above left: The opening of the new premises in 1968 with left to right: Abraham Bellow, Irwin Bellow (Lord Bellwin) and The Lord Mayor of Leeds, Alderman Turnbull.*

to the growth of the company could hardly be over emphasised, began travelling throughout Europe and the USA to keep abreast of the latest developments in the garment machine field. This resulted in the first of many agencies to sell foreign built machines to supplement the expanding range of Bellow's own manufacture.

The first overseas representation was for the Strobel range of Blindstitch Felling machines in 1927, to be followed in 1929 by the franchise for Maimin Cutting Machines. Those agencies would still be flourishing in the 21st century.

Business grew over the years, more types of machines were manufactured in Leeds, more overseas representations were added and the sales organisation was built up throughout the country.

In 1938 the first branch office was opened in London to cope with the ever increasing volume of business, to be followed in 1939 by a Manchester branch. The second world war now caused a stop to future expansion and from 1939-45 the factory was devoted to the manufacture of aircraft components and anti-aircraft gun parts.

The manufacture of garment machinery began again in 1945 at the end of the war. The original premises in Grafton Street became too small and a move was made to a 50,000 sq ft factory in Ellerby Lane, whilst the administration offices remained in Grafton Street. New machines such as Blindstitch, Work Transporters of all types, Cloth Spreaders, Ticket Attaching machines, Cloth Shrinking machines and a host of others now appeared in the manufacturing programme, and a healthy export business was developed.

*Top right: Ted Hyman and Prime Minister, Harold Wilson at an exhibition in Moscow in 1966.*

In 1948, under the Managing Directorship of the founder's son Irwin Bellow (later Lord Bellwin) who had joined the business after the war, the firm became a public company and a policy was introduced of expanding the sales and service network.

A year earlier, the year in which Ted Hyman, later joint managing director, joined the company as a trainee executive, the company had become sole importers and distributors of the Pfaff range of industrial sewing machines. The remarkable quality and design of the Pfaff machines soon began to be accepted by all branches of the garment manufacturing industry. The machines were competitively priced and backed by the after-sales service in which the company was now specialising. Sales of these machines grew steadily, and created a business relationship between Pfaff and Bellow's which would have significant consequences many years down the line.

The Directors of the company, who had been joined by Mr Bellows second son, Marshall Bellow in 1956, now travelled the world to keep abreast of developments in machinery for the many industries for which the company now catered, developing exports markets and gaining new representations such as those for the USA's Automatic Steam Products Corporation, Schmetz needles, Hoffman Presses, Gratech Teva Servo Cutters and many others.

In 1968, after a disastrous fire at Grafton Street, the company moved into new purpose built headquarters, show rooms and offices adjoining the factory in Ellerby Lane. For the first time the company had outstanding premises for exhibitions, conferences and seminars.

The following year the company merged with the Staflex organisation, Ted Hyman and Marshall Bellow becoming joint managing directors of the Bellow Group. It now became necessary to wind down the manufacturing side of the company when it became clear that the firm would never become a major manufacturer itself and that its main expertise was in selling and servicing the equipment which it supplied on an exclusive basis to the garment and allied trades all over the UK.

Amongst the new faces who now joined the company would be Colin Pinder and Mike Stone who both subsequently became board members.

In May 1978 the company severed its links with Staflex and became a wholly owned subsidiary of GM Pfaff AG which Bellow's had by then represented for over 30 years. Irwin Bellow was appointed Chairman with his brother Marshall as joint Managing Director with Ted Hyman.

The following year Irwin Bellow, a former Leeds Grammar School student and a graduate from Leeds University became Lord Bellwin and joined Margaret Thatcher's government, later becoming Minister of State for Local Government. As Irwin Bellow, Lord Bellwin had served as a Leeds councillor from 1969

and was Leader of Leeds City Council from 1975 to 1979. During that time he had sold more than 3,000 council houses to their tenants. By 1978 his tight control of local spending had given Leeds ratepayers the lowest metropolitan district rate in the country.

Marshall Bellow now took over as Chairman of the company, with Ted Hyman as Managing Director, positions which both would hold until their retirement in the 1990s. By then Mike Stone, who had joined the company as an apprentice engineer, had worked his way through the company to become Managing Director and later Chairman. Another notable name in this period was Colin Pinder who had served as Finance Director from the mid 1970s until his retirement at the end of the 1990s.

Irwin Bellow's son, Stephen, had joined the family firm in 1974 though left after just eight years to start his own business. Stephen Bellow rejoined the business in 1999 after buying it back from its owners Pfaff. At the same time Lord Bellwin returned to the company as its Chairman after an absence of more than 20 years; he continued in that position up until his death in 2001 at the age of 78.

At the start of the 21st century the company's main markets would be Mauritius, Jordan, India, Pakistan Bangladesh the Gulf states and, to a lesser extent today, the UK. The company has built a reputation for being able to supply complete 'turnkey' projects providing machinery and know-how to start up an entire factory.

Who could have guessed in 1919 just what an extraordinary legacy Abraham Bellow would leave to his descendants?

*Top right: Lord Bellwin, formerly Irwin Bellow. Left: The current Directors from left to right: Andrew Gardiner, Malcolm Price (Managing Director), Derek Cottle and Stephen Bellow (Chairman).*

# *The electrical age*

Nothing, absolutely nothing so marked the history of the 20th century, and particularly its last half, as the arrival of electrical household goods at affordable prices. Most people over the age of fifty reading this book will be able to recall their excitement at the delivery of the first washing machine, fridge, television and video recorder. Indeed perhaps it is television more than any other electrical appliance which has created the greatest changes to our world.

But where to buy those miracles of technology which have made our lives so much more interesting over the last half century or so? For Leeds folk the answer has very often been the firm of Jones of Oakwood Ltd, a firm which today, amongst its other interests, runs Leeds' prestigious Sony Centre Galleria. But the Jones electrical business has been around far far longer than the Japanese electronics industry, indeed Jones' has been in business in Leeds since well before even the first experimental television transmissions were made.

Jones of Oakwood started life in 1917. Fred Jones, born in 1874, was working as a plumber from a garage in Back Road, Oakwood Parade, Roundhay Road. In 1920 Fred struck up a friendship with Welham's Decorators on the Parade and together they decided to start a plumbing business in Leeds. That company, which later became known as Jones Leeds Ltd, employed 20 plumbers and were contracted to do all the maintenance for Tetley's Brewery.

Continuing success seemed inevitable, but in 1923 the foreman walked out and took the Tetley's contract with him. As a result of that lost contract the business went under and Fred Jones returned to his smaller business premises, the garage behind Oakwood Parade.

But that was far from being the end of the story, it was only its beginning. By 1935 Fred's son, Albert Edward Jones, 'Eddie', born in 1901, was running F Jones & Son Ltd. Eddie decide that he wanted to get out onto Oakwood Parade and occupy a more a visible position. The opportunity came as a result of

***Below:*** *The company's first premises pictured in 1897.*

1946 Bailey's secured Rowland's release from the Navy and he returned to his apprenticeship. A few months or so before his father Eddie's death in 1948, at the early age of 47, Rowland left Bailey's and went into the family business. Rowland's brother Leslie was by then serving his own apprenticeship in the company as a plumber. In 1949 the firm changed its name from F Jones & Son (Oakwood) Ltd to Jones of Oakwood Ltd; Rowland now began to develop the electrical contracting side of the business.

In the 1950s, when technical development was limited and the post war years of austerity still lingered, the main problem the business faced was getting enough stock to make sufficient profit to make a living which would support two families. One promising area was that of television. Though the first television broadcasts had occurred before the war, BBC television broadcasting had not resumed until peace had returned to Europe. Even so there was relatively little interest in the new fangled goggle-box until the coronation of Queen Elizabeth II in 1953. Those who watched the event live on television would never forget it. The many who had no television crowded into the homes of the few who owned one and decided that they too would like to own this marvel of the new Elizabethan age. That demand was further stoked by the advent of ITV in the mid 1950s which brought a new, brash and immensely popular element to the somewhat stuffy approach to broadcasting which had been Lord Reith's legacy to the BBC. ITV brought advertising to the

competition for trade between two dry cleaners on opposite sides of the road. Both shops were owned by Smiths, who, realising that one was superfluous, offered Eddie his choice of premises. That choice of the south side was made on the toss of a coin. That random flip of a penny proved to be very fortunate; the north side of the parade had over a period of some 15 years been bought up by a building contractor, Henry Lax, as shops became vacant. Henry Lax would not sell any of his property, which prevented any expansion or development. Had Eddie chosen the premises on the north side the subsequent expansion of the shop and business would never have been possible.

The electrical side of the business began in 1947. Eddie's eldest son, Rowland, had as a young man, been apprenticed to local electricians NG Bailey. In 1944 Rowland went into the Navy as an electrician serving on mine sweepers in the North Sea. In

*This page:* *Views of Oakwood Parade in the 1950s.*

small screen (the first of which was for Gibbs SR toothpaste) and also advertised television itself. Jones of Oakwood wanted to move into television, but they had to become a recognised agent. In 1961 they applied to Bush, Murphy and Pye but were refused by all three as those agencies were in the possession of another dealer in Harehills called Ainleys.

It seemed a critical opportunity was being missed. Demand for television was increasing every day despite the high cost and the concept of rental became a main factor in the way customers could obtain TV. Jones wanted to be in that market.

But all was not lost. The next year changed everything. Sidney Simmons, a former Lord Mayor of Leeds and owner of an electrical business in Dewsbury Road was passing the Jones' shop on his way to the bank and offered to sell them his business. This was a well-established shop that held all the electrical agencies and had a complete service department. The offer could not be refused and Jones of Oakwood Ltd was now in a position to trade in television. By 1974 they would not only have the original agencies

they had acquired from Sydney Simmons but would also have obtained the prized Panasonic agency.

As the electrical side of the business grew and the company's reputation was established the brothers were asked to set up a local buying group with other local businesses. This was soon formed and would eventually have a large influence on the company. The buying power of the group, which eventually expanded to include over 40 dealers throughout the West Riding, helped to obtain better prices for the group members and enabled those dealers to compete with the big discounters coming into the markets.

The buying office and administration was all done from Rowland's office at Oakwood. As the buying group's reputation grew interest was aroused in London and Rowland was invited to become a director of the Voluntary National buying group, CIH, which had offices in London. This involvement benefited the company and escalated their development in the mid

*Top: Jones shop front early 1960s.*
*Above: A Jones of Oakwood Ltd advertisement from 1962.*

1970s when there was a definite shortage of televisions as having a major influence in the group enabled them to be very close to the manufacturers.

Before then however, in 1969, Leslie and Rowland Jones had the chance to buy land at the rear of the Oakwood Parade premises. The land was needed for parking and was bought from a Miss Nettleton, the daughter of a builder, for £350. A few years later, when the Government began sheltered housing schemes, it was decided to offer the land for the building of retirement homes. Twelve flats were built with 1,500 sq ft of storage beneath. The land was leased back to Jones' for a peppercorn rent of £10 per annum for 99 years. Jones' now had an increased amount of storage space available at almost no cost to themselves. The extra space now meant that expansion was possible. In 1970 when the premises of Dewhursts the Butchers, in the adjacent shop, was put up for sale, Jones' was able to buy these premises too.

By 1975 with a sales force of ten, a total staff of 24 and two sets of premises the shop needed a refit. The company joined 'Expert' a European group of 1400 independent retailers from 11 countries that had strict guidelines on house colours, shop-fitting and logos. Jones' had joined Expert in order for the company to improve and maintain its standards and image in the face of growing competition from larger retailers. The Oakwood shop was refurbished using the Expert profile: five men arrived from Hamburg, bringing all they needed with them. The task was completed in four days - comedian, the late Les Dawson, opened the new shop in 1975 for the price of a 26" colour

**Left:** *The Moor Allerton store.*
**Below:** *The Head Office in 1986.*

television. Les arrived at 2 pm for a two hour engagement, but stayed until 7pm when the final customers left.

The next opportunity that came the brother's way was the closing down of Nathan Bake Ltd, the next door grocers. The acquisition of that shop gave Jones' the space to expand their range and when the off-licence next door to the grocers too became vacant the offer seemed too good to resist, enabling Jones' to stock an increasingly large range of both home electronics and domestic appliances.

During the early 1970s Leslie's son Andrew, and Rowland's son Martin had joined the business; starting at the very bottom of the ladder they set out to learn the trade, in keeping with their fathers' firm conviction that they should learn every aspect of the business. That learning included experiencing the good times and the bad. Unfortunately in 1976 the contracting side of the business was badly affected when the construction industry was going through a bad patch and the plumbing side was closed down, though the electrical contracting department would struggle on until 1990. For the next ten years however the company made far better progress in the electronics and appliance business with Andrew and Martin being eventually given more and more responsibility.

In 1980 the company heard that Sainsbury's was opening a supermarket on a site on the Ring Road. This was pursued over a two-year period and in spite of strong competition from multiples, such as Comet and Dixons, Jones of Oakwood was

able to obtain the lease to open at the Sainsbury Moor Allerton site next to the supermarket.

Ventures such as a large store in Morley and also a large concession within Woods Music shop in Bradford operated successfully for a number of years before both closing in the mid-1980s allowing them to focus on different projects.

In 1982, in view of Jones' progress in marketing, the company approached Sony with a proposal for an exclusive Sony Centre in Leeds. Jones' bid succeeded against strong opposition from other retailers; Jones' Leeds Sony Centre was a triumph and a second Jones' Sony Centre opened in Wakefield in 1988.

Meanwhile, Leslie Jones had retired from the business in 1985 for health reasons and Rowland would stand down in the early

**Top left:** *Les Dawson opens the new shop in 1975.*
**Left:** *The Jones family pictured in the early 1980s. From Left to right: Andrew, Leslie, Martin and Rowland.*
**Below:** *The Lord Mayor of Leeds at this time, Councillor Sydney Symmonds, pictured with Rowland Jones, (left), and Leslie Jones, (right), at the opening of the new store in Morley in 1985.*

head office had been acquired to accommodate the ever increasing levels of demand for stock. At the start of the new century both Sony Centres were totally refurbished and enlarged, helping Jones' to sell even more of the latest futuristic 'state of the art' Sony products. The Sony Centre in Leeds is the largest in Europe and had recently gained 'galleria' status following on from similar status being awarded to Harrods and one other store in the London area. Leeds' Sony Centre Galleria could truly boast to being the jewel in Sony's crown, its flagship store in the UK. But that was not all. In 2001 a new commercial department of Jones' opened; the new division of the company would supply top brand electrical equipment to businesses, schools, universities, hospitals, hotels and local authorities.

Andrew and Martin have always seen their quality staff as their biggest strength. Training plays a key part in their success and in November of 2002 they were presented with the coveted Investors in People award.

Today the Directors believe that as long as they move with the times, continue to invest in the business and their staff and offer the latest products and technology at the right prices, the future is bright. No doubt they are right; the 20th century saw the arrival of so many marvels into our homes who can doubt that the 21st century will see even more miracles of technology.

*Top right: The Sony Centre in Wakefield.*
*Above left: The flagship Sony Centre Galleria store in Leeds.*
*Top left: A recent view of the firm's Oakwood store with the head office on floors one and two. Below: Joint Managing Directors, Andrew Jones (left) and Martin Jones.*

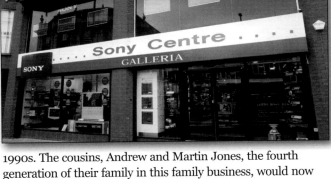

1990s. The cousins, Andrew and Martin Jones, the fourth generation of their family in this family business, would now become joint heads of the company.

In 1996, now led by Andrew and Martin, the company began a new venture which proved to be extremely successful: they began offering 'affinity deals' to large blue chip companies and financial organisations. This involved developing, for the staff of those companies, a scheme whereby employees would be sent an 80 page brochure of electrical products priced very advantageously. This was used as a 'perk' by the organisation involved to their staff. Over 1.5 million brochures are now sent out each year to 46 different companies. Such affinity deals would soon equate to more than 40 per cent of the company's turnover.

With such innovations Jones of Oakwood Ltd continued to expand, and by the early years of the new millennium was employing over 85 staff in its various 6 departments. In 2000 Jones of Oakwood was awarded the 'Gold Award' for outstanding service in the Electrical Retail Industry. There would be a substantial call centre in the first floor offices at Oakwood Parade, and trade via the Internet was increasing daily. A large warehouse, totalling 45,000 sq ft, close to the

# No 1 for coach holidays

Gosh! Trips on coaches aren't like they used to be. In 2002 the renowned Wallace Arnold Group based in Leeds launched the ultimate in luxury coach travel. The new £2.5 million 'Grand Tourer' fleet introduced a level of luxury normally only found in the first class section of intercontinental aircraft such as sumptuous leather seating and an integral lounge. Not surprisingly the first year's programme quickly sold out for all its 27 destinations, spanning France, Austria, Portugal, Holland, Belgium, Russia, Italy and Spain.

Costing a quarter of a million pounds each of the distinctive black and gold coaches feature just 36 seats instead of the usual 48, providing almost 50 per cent more leg room as well as double-glazed, tinted windows, television monitors and a multi track sound system with individual headsets.

Wallace Arnold's roots can be traced back to the Leeds of 1912 when Robert Barr bought his first vehicle, a four ton, solid-tyred Karrier bus which was used as a lorry during the week

and for 'charabanc' trips to the countryside at weekends. These days of course it's only the very oldest amongst us that still call a coach a chara. And strictly speaking the Karrier bus wasn't actually a chara anyway: the original charabanc was a horse drawn vehicle usually open to the elements with benches or 'bancs' going across the whole width of the vehicle. By the 1920s motor charabancs were a common sight. Robert Barr advertised himself as a 'Motor charabanc proprietor and removal and haulage contractor,' but his focus would soon shift overwhelmingly to coach travel.

Expansion began in 1926 when Robert Barr bought out the Leeds-based charabanc operators Wallace Cunningham and Arnold Crowe.

***Top left:*** *Robert Barr, founder of the Barr and Wallace Arnold Trust.*
***Above:*** *A Wallace Arnold letter dated 1921 and addressed to a Mr Barker asking for advice on how many seats he would like reserved for a trip to the London Motor Show.* ***Below:*** *An early 'bus' from 1919, a 28 seat solid tyred Karrier.*

By 1930 Robert Barr's Wallace Arnold coach fleet comprised 15 vehicles, and by the outbreak of war in 1939 that number had doubled to 30.

In times of war the country needed coaches. At the start of the second world war the government requisitioned 12 of the company's coaches to be used as ambulances and troop carriers.

For the duration of the war any further plans for expansion had to be put on hold. But the year after the war ended Wallace Arnold was able to put 46 new coaches on the road. The popularity of coach travel was greatly enhanced by the fact that for folk in Leeds, as everywhere else, there was a two year waiting list for a new car.

But Leeds would not be the only focus of the company's marketing policy in those austere post war times. In the years immediately following the end of the war the firm began offering visiting Americans a choice of four tours of London.

Wallace Arnold also offered visiting Americans 'delightful' tours of Yorkshire, with tourists being offered a package which included rail travel from London to Leeds, where they stayed overnight before being introduced to the glories of the Yorkshire countryside.

So involved with the American market did the company now become that it even had brochures distributed in North America with its prices marked in dollars. In 1949 a 14 day tour of the Scottish Highlands cost $190.00.

Nor was Wallace Arnold only involved in coach tours. In the 1950s the company bought two bus companies in Leeds: Kippax & District Ltd and the Farsley Omnibus Company.

But the 1950s were the golden years of coach travel. At the height of the 1950s boom Wallace Arnold was able to offer eight different continental tours. For less than £40 it was possible to set off on coach trips to Switzerland, France, Austria, Italy, Holland or Spain.

How many readers recall starting their holidays from the Calls Coach Station behind the Corn Exchange in those years we wonder? How many readers recall being decked out in their best holiday clothes for a trip to the seaside armed with a packet of sandwiches wrapped in grease proof paper all aquiver to see the sea?

**Top left:** *Schofields of Leeds on their staff outing 1923.*
**Top right:** *A 1926 invoice for a trip to Ulleskelf, costing £3 2s 6d. At this time storage, removals and overhauls were amongst the other services offered by the company.*
**Above left:** *Robert Barr (far right) poses with a number of happy passengers about to board the Leeds Mercury escorted motor tour in 1937. The Leyland Tiger coach pictured was requisitioned by the Air Force in 1939.*
**Below:** *A Wallace Arnold Leyland Tiger PS1, 1930s.*

No televisions on board then to entertain us. 'We had to make our own entertainment in those days' is the often heard refrain of the older generation to today's computer-obsessed youngsters. And didn't we just? Is there anyone over the age of fifty who hasn't spent hours of a sun-filled summer's day singing about those blessed ten green bottles hanging so precariously on the wall? We may have enjoyed it but pity the poor coach driver who heard the same old words day after day. The drivers certainly deserved their tip when the hat was passed round at the end of the trip. Looking back it's a wonder those long suffering coach driver's didn't stop at the first lay-by they came to and threaten to hang us all on a wall if we didn't find another song to sing! 'OK, very sorry driver, all together now...On Ilkley Moor baht 'at....'. 'Grrrrrr'.

At least some of the coach drivers had one consolation; they got to see the world - well Europe anyway. Though two of the continental tours were only available once a year others operated up to nine times over the holiday season. More locally, day trips from such places as Scarborough could be had for as little as 1s 3d (6p) for a short circular tour, whilst for 13 shillings (65p) trippers could enjoy a whole day out at Stokesley and the Cleveland Hills.

The company continued to grow throughout the 1950s as Robert Barr bought up other carriers, both in Leeds and Scarborough. In the mid 1950s the company was able to claim that it was carrying more than 25,000 holiday makers every year.

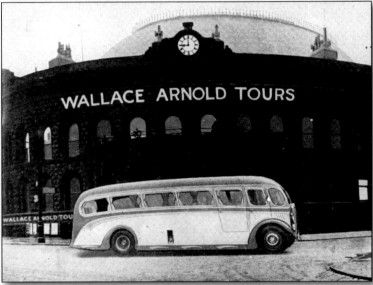

Nor were summer trips the only thing. The company now became one of the first British coach operators to offer low-cost off-season holidays so opening up a new and growing market providing cheaper holidays to those who could not afford high season prices or who preferred to avoid the crowds. With schemes like these it was not surprising that in 1961 Wallace Arnold announced a record number of bookings.

By 1961 the company's continental holiday programme now included not only coach tours, which had by now been extended to Norway, but also included holidays by air, sea and rail.

The increasing national prosperity however brought with it challenges for Wallace Arnold. As car ownership increased

*Top: There was a pent-up demand in Britain when the war ended as this queue outside the Corn Exchange illustrates. They were waiting to book Wallace Arnold coastal express services.*
*Above: A montage of the Corn Exchange, the Wallace Arnold Tours sign and a 1940s coach. Left: Outings to the coast by Working Mens Clubs were a popular fea-ture of the early 1950s as shown by this splendid line of Wallace Arnold coaches ready for departure.*

rapidly in the 1970s there began a steady decline in day trips; fortunately, also due to increased prosperity, the demand for continental holidays began to expand rapidly too.

Wallace Arnold's continental tour programme for 1971 had offered 38,000 seats, the following year this was increased by more than 10% to 42,000 seats.

The decade of the 1970s ended with Wallace Arnold carrying some 250,000 people, ten times more passengers than it had in the 1950s, and covering many millions of passenger miles each year.

In 1975 the company reached an agreement with operators in Paris and Florence for a jointly operated express coach service linking the cities of London, Paris, Lyon, Turin, Genoa, Florence and Rome. Despite European red tape this remarkable cross-Europe service was launched in 1977 and ran once a week during the summer months with an end to end journey time of 37 hours for a return fare of £63.

With the success of this London to Rome service Wallace Arnold now set its sights on a plum destination - Moscow - then still firmly behind the iron curtain. Negotiations were concluded in 1977 with a joint service with Soviet operators due to start in 1979.

Meanwhile the company's 'Dream Holidays for the Elderly' was becoming increasingly important, though in 1979, recognising that those advanced in age are not necessarily 'elderly', the programme was rebranded as 'Supersaver Holidays for the Older Holidaymaker'.

But not all passengers travelled all the way by coach. Lining up with P&O cruises in 1980 cruise holidays now became a focus of the company's attention. Wallace Arnold launched a series of European holidays which combined coach travel with cruising on the P&O's Canberra and Oriana liners. From just £364 clients could enjoy a 12 day holiday, taking a coach from Britain to Nice and returning by sea, or, if they preferred, the other way around.

The 1980s would be a time of change in the coach industry and a new strategy was devised by the company, a programme summed up in its 1987 annual report:

'Our strategy is to offer good quality, value for money services; operate the most modern fleet of coaches in the country and to provide a highly efficient booking service'.

Those objectives have never been deviated from. Investment and reinvestment continued with the company never content

*Top:* Wallace Arnold's Leeds booking office in 1953.
*Below left:* A happy group of early 1950s holiday makers, do you recognise anybody?
*Below:* During the 1950s the company owned two bus companies in Leeds - The Kippax and District and Farsley Omnibus. A bus belonging to the latter company is seen below at Stanningley Bottom showing a family complete with collapsible push chair.

to rest on its laurels. The reservation system for example had been fully computerised since 1982, but from 1985 a new on-line system now gave travel agents direct access. The system was further updated at a cost of almost a million pounds in 1989.

The late 1980s were an especially good period for the company which continued to improve its performance and earned the accolade of 'Top Coach Operator' in both 1988 and 1989. Those accolades would continue to come with the company being awarded the title 'Best British and European Tour Programme 1995/96'.

Despite the economic recession which arrived at the start of the 1990s Wallace Arnold still retained its extensive and innovative programme, its investment in new coaches and - most critically - its profitability. And despite the stagnant economy some areas of the market still provided new growth opportunities such as tours of Ireland through a combination of coach/sea and coach/air holidays.

On the continent the majority of holidays continued to be run using the company's own vehicles, although that did not prevent new links with France's prestigious high speed train the TGV which whisked holiday-makers south from Paris after being taken there by coach from Britain. And of course, with the opening of the Channel Tunnel, holidays were now promoted using the Eurostar train service.

As an alternative to those who preferred to spend their time travelling by coach through France in order to reach Spain, Wallace Arnold now also offered coach links to a new ferry/cruise service run by P&O running between Portsmouth and Bilbao.

Meanwhile back in Britain the company was investing in hotels to ensure that it could offer guaranteed

*Top left: A 1950s Plaxton bodied tourer.*
*Top right: A 1960s Plaxton bodied tourer.*
*Above right: One of Wallace Arnold's new Sunsundegui coaches.*
*Right: The Wallace Arnold fleet circles Headingley cricket ground before transporting the supporters of Leeds Rhinos to Wembley for the 1999 Challenge Cup final.*

agents and the travel industry in the United Kingdom.

quality standards. The Grand Hotel in Exmouth, the Broadway Park at Sandown on the Isle of Wight, the Burlington at Eastbourne, the Savoy at Bournemouth and the Trecarn at Babbacombe would soon become familiar to those who sought out the highest quality in food, accommodation and entertainment. To those initial acquisitions would be added other hotels, not least the company's first Scottish hotel, bought in 2001, the 84 bedroom Fife Arms at Braemar, Royal Deeside taking the total number of Wallace Arnold hotels to eight.

In 1997, backed by funds from equity partner 3i, the business benefited from a successful management buy-out enabling the company to plan its future independently.

In an unprecedented achievement in 2002 Wallace Arnold was voted Britain's 'best coach operator' being given awards by no fewer than seven different bodies representing customers travel

Hardly surprising when in 2002 Wallace Arnold announced it was to introduce no fewer than 51 new coaches worth over £9 million to its already modern fleet.

Those new coaches included 36 from coachwork builder Jonckheere, all based on Volvo chassis bodies, 10 of which were the special 'Grand Tourer versions which offer the ultimate in luxury coach travel such as reclining leather seats and a separate rear lounge. Of the remainder, nine would be from coachbuilder Plaxton and six from Spanish coachwork specialists Sunsundegui, the latter appearing in the group's 225 strong fleet for the very first time.

In the opening years of the new millennium The Wallace Arnold Group could claim without fear of contradiction to be Britain's No 1 coach tour operator with its three operating companies, more than 1,000 employees, over half a million customers ever year and a turnover of more than a £100 million annually from its 8 hotels, 25 travel agencies and 225 luxury coaches.

It is all a long way from Robert Barr's early trips with his solid-tyred 'chara'. Although many decades may have passed since then the company still maintains a belief in the traditions passed on by Robert Barr: the tradition of always providing the very best in customer care still remains at the forefront of company policy.

*Top left and left: The impressive 'Grand Tourer' coach fleet. Top right: Wallace Arnold's Marketing Manager Gordon Durrans relaxes in the Grand Tourer's lounge with Volvo's Jenny Cooke. Above left: Ken Meddles, Chief Executive of The Wallace Arnold Group.*

# *Braking lights*

For more than a century WABCO based at the Beacon Works in Texas Street, Morley, has consistently pursued a single objective - 'to enhance safety'. Never resting on its laurels, in recent times the company's lifeblood has been the development of new, efficient electronic vehicle control systems to guard against human error - systems which enhance the control of vehicles and performance by using technology to the best advantage.

With plants and agents in over 30 countries spanning five continents WABCO covers the world's automotive industry. That global presence has allowed the company to develop close contact with the industry it serves and to understand its needs and requirements. A wealth of knowledge is directly channelled into the development of tomorrow's innovative solutions, continuing a process which began many generations ago.

*Above: Founders, William Ackroyd (left) and William Best. Below: Morley Main Colliery situated in Albert Road shortly before its demolition, circa 1909.*

The WABCO story begins in the 19th century with William Ackroyd and William Best who founded Ackroyd and Best, the forerunner of today's company.

William Ackroyd, a mining engineer born in 1849, came from a wealthy background of local industrialists whilst William Best, born in Pudsey in 1846, had begun work at Morley Main Colliery as a pit boy at the age of 10 and eventually had risen to become Lamp Foreman. William Best was a creative genius when it came to lamp design; the two Williams met when William Ackroyd assumed control of Morley Main where he quickly recognised Best's abilities.

WABCO Leeds owes its existence however to a disaster which had taken place more than 20 years earlier: a fatal explosion at Morley Main on 7th October 1872 which took the lives of 34 men and boys. That disaster was the catalyst which had prompted William Best, then a lamp man at the mine, to begin developing new, safer lamps; though it would be another two decades before he and Ackroyd would take out their first patent.

Ackroyd and Best took out 12 patents before starting large scale production and by both selling and renting their lamps were before long able to boast that 250,000 of their lamps were in use despite the strong competition from Leeds where the Karl Wolf company had three times as many of its lamps in circulation.

Ackroyd and Best opened their first factory when they rented a building in High Street, Morley, in 1896; it became known as the Hembrigg Lamp Works. In 1897 a limited company was formed with a share capital value of £25,000 and with Ackroyd and Best as respectively its Chairman and General Manager. Best became a director in 1898 but only remained on the board for a single year.

The company had moved to the Perseverance Works in 1902, and would stay there until 1911. During that time many more patents were taken out dealing with miners' lamps. It was incidentally not possible to patent the miners' safety lamp itself - famously that had been invented by Sir Humphrey Davy in 1813, and Davy had refused to patent his invention on the grounds that it should be freely available for the benefit of all mankind. Consequently it was only possible to patent improvements in construction and ignition systems to the basic Davy design.

In 1908, after years of bickering and conflicts of interest, William Best was dismissed by the company, along with three of his sons who were then employed by the firm, after it was discovered that they had in effect set up a rival firm 'the Best Contracting Company'. William continued to work on the development of miners' lamps, and even as late as 1916, at the age of 70, he obtained Ministry approval for the design of a new gauze-less lamp for use in mines. William Best died at his home on Morley in 1932.

In 1911 the company moved from Perseverance Works to the new, purpose-built Beacon Works, where the production of miners' lamps continued. Then in 1914, just after the outbreak of the first world war, heat-resistant glass tubes for lamps, which until then had been supplied by a German company, became unobtainable: in 1915 the company added its own glass works to the Beacon Works site.

At about that time, to aid the war effort the factory became 'controlled' and work began on the manufacture of munitions. This entailed the purchase of more machinery and more land on which to extend the brass foundry. A rifle range was also set up in the cellars and by 1915 the company had purchased 13,500 cartridges for use there.

*Top left:* Beacon Works whilst under construction, 1911.
*Above:* A brochure of the Ackroyd and Best Safety Lamp.
*Below:* The Hailwood factory in the 1920s.

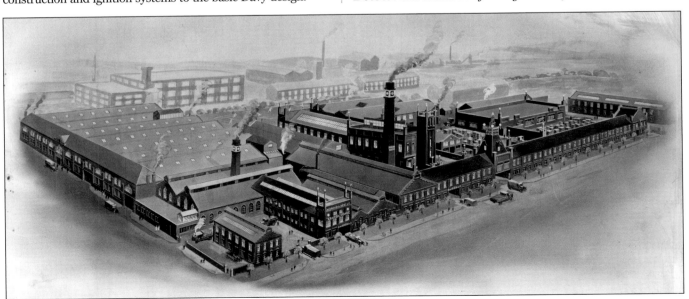

The production of miners' lamps increased rapidly during the war years in line with the increasing demand for fuel from the coal mines. When 'home-produced' glass finally came on stream it ensured the continuity of lamp manufacture; and with the restrictions imposed on the importation of miners' lamp glass, a restriction which would remain in force up to five years after the end of the war in 1918, the company also had to meet the glass needs of its competitors.

In 1919 company General Manager Ernest Hailwood visited the continent and made arrangements for a number of foreign workers to come to Morley to work in the glass works. These people from the continent: Russia, Germany and Czechoslovakia, possessed special skills not previously available in Britain; the new workers included artists, glassblowers and mixers used to handling and dealing with every kind of glass making process. As such they were ideally qualified to work on a complex range of products - particularly advertising products - in glass. But not just glass.

William Ackroyd died in 1920, the year the company began a Mint operation producing an East African 50 cent (one shilling) coin. Meanwhile the range of glass products continued to expand. In the 1920s the range included industrial and medical glassware, roof lights, gas and oil globes, illumination glassware, cut glass, advertising and lettered glassware and decorated illuminating glassware.

The mixing of compounds was carried out in a building later occupied by the engineering department. The process was a

closely guarded secret known only to the mixer, and not even communicated to the people who actually mixed the materials. They included not only sand but lead, Ash Regulus of Antimony, manganese, gold, chloride of silver, arsenic and even uranium.

Expansion became the watchword. In addition to a showroom at the Beacon Works other showrooms were now opened in London and Glasgow whilst agencies were established in Canada, Mexico and Spain.

*Top:* Glass blowing in the main glassworks at Beacon Works. ***Above:*** Glass blowing, showing how the process relied on a great deal of teamwork.

Decorative and coloured glass products ranging from items with industrial and safety applications to decorative products for the home - all extremely difficult to manufacture - were added to the company's range . In 1934 the company would even manufacture the Belisha Beacons, named after the then Minister of Transport, used to mark pedestrian crossing points. The orange Belisha beacon was developed following much research work to established the best method of production. The one chosen was a three-ply glass construction consisting of an inner white opal layer, a yellow middle layer and an outer layer of clear glass. Although they were made in Morley, surprisingly, the local council refused to erect them in the town. In the same period it is also believed that the prototypes of Halifax inventor Percy Shaw's 'Cats eyes' road studs were made by Hailwood and Ackroyd, which also patented its own similar reflectors. The company is also said to have designed and erected the first set of traffic lights in Leeds.

As the company's product range increased in the 1920s the production of miners' safety lamps was scaled down. There was much talk of the Davy-style lamp being replaced by an electric-powered lamp, not least because many miners suffered from an eye condition thought to be caused by the oil-filled Davy lamp. Although the company had flirted with electric lamps as early as 1912, Hailwood nevertheless happily used the eye condition as a selling point for the company's oil lamps, claiming that the condition was far more prevalent where the electric lights were used. Despite that assertion, electric lamps gradually replaced oil lamps, though the latter would still have a role because of their ability to give a warning of gas in a mine.

The company name was changed in 1927 to Hailwood and Ackroyd, and it would continue making glass products through to 1979.

Ernest Arthur Hailwood had joined the company in 1897 as Company Secretary and remained in that position until William Best's dismissal following which he had combined the roles of Company Secretary and General Manager. Hailwood was an entrepreneur and much of the company's development, especially after William Ackroyd's death, was as a direct result of action taken by him. During his years with the firm a wider range of products was introduced and patented, including hand-held lamps, lamp locking devices and lamp ignition devices enabling lamps to be safely re-ignited underground.

*Top left: Beacon Works Lamp fitting shop, the damaged lamps (bottom left) were returned for refurbishment under the continuous hire system. Above: View of the Iron Turning Shop during the early part of the occupation of Beacon Works. Right: Early company transport, 1915.*

The 30 years during which Ernest Hailwood ran the business were remarkable ones for the company; his strong personality had in part been responsible for the departure of William Best and his family. Hailwood himself however was a family man too and all his five children became involved with the company: especially his four daughters. Gertrude Hailwood was the first woman in England to obtain a BSc in glass technology and joined the company in 1934 as a materials analyst. Muriel Hailwood qualified as Morley's first female aeroplane pilot in 1936 and was employed to write the company's advertising material: in 1934 she had written 'We're a happy crowd' a song intended to be sung by miners, with song sheets, featuring a picture of the Hailwood Miner's Lamp on the cover, circulated to every miner in the country. Meanwhile her sister Sylvia studied at Leeds College of Art and Industrial Design, she produced several designs taken up by the company whilst the fourth sister, Mary Hailwood RA, an accomplished artist, drew many of the sketches used by the company for publicity purposes.

Vilified in the local press for his outspoken right wing political views 'Hailwood the Hustler' as he became

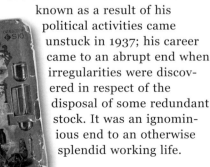

known as a result of his political activities came unstuck in 1937; his career came to an abrupt end when irregularities were discovered in respect of the disposal of some redundant stock. It was an ignominious end to an otherwise splendid working life.

War work again became the company's focus during the dark days of

1939-45. In the 1950s however the company went into the engineering industry and from then on greater emphasis was placed on that side of the business. In that decade the company began taking on sub-contract machining work to supplement the decline in the demand for its miners' lamps and a tractor hydraulic line was set up.

In 1965 Hailwood and Ackroyd Ltd became part of Clayton Dewandre, the largest manufacturer of braking equipment for the UK truck industry. The change in ownership brought with it an influx of new products,

*Top left: EA Hailwood. Top right:Beacon Works Showroom. Left: A Hailwood and Ackroyd catalogue. Above: An early Hailwood and Ackroyd Ltd exhibition stand.*

this time brake components for the automotive industry, some of which would continue to be manufactured for the next four decades. The production of miners' lamps, the company's original product, now came to an end.

In 1977 Clayton Dewandre merged with WABCO, a wholly owned division of American Standard. The merger brought new ideas in its wake for products aimed mainly at the motor vehicle market. At the beginning of the 1980s the company would invest heavily in computer-controlled machinery and in products such as the piston vacuum pump were added to the range. The glassworks meanwhile was closed down in 1979 followed by the closure of the foundry in 1985.

With the closure of Clayton Dewandre's operation in Lincoln in 1986, production of a large range of its products which until then had been manufactured in Lincoln was now transferred to Leeds and to the Howley Park factory, a short distance from the Beacon Works, which had been involved in making spring brakes was now turned over to making compressors.

In 1991 the company name was changed from Hailwood and Ackroyd Ltd to WABCO, completing the change from the early days to the present time. Additional product ranges were introduced during the 1990s: air dryers were transferred from WABCO UK's sister company WABCO Austria, the development of the new Group Quad Valve finally came to fruition and manufacture began . Pressure modulators and electrically driven vacuum pumps would be the last new products of the 20th century to go into volume production.

WABCO is one of the operating divisions of The American Standard Family of Companies totalling 61,000 employees in more than 20 countries worldwide.

Today, after more than one hundred years of manufacturing in Morley, WABCO and its employees can look back with pride, having saved countless lives by their innovation and expertise.

**Top left:** *WABCO Vacuum Pumps.* **Above left:** *Air Dryers.* **Left:** *A WABCO Quad Valve.* **Below:** *The factory today.*

# *From Bayeaux to Beijing*

International construction and management consultants Turner & Townsend's appointment as Project and Cost Managers for the Leeds Supertram project confirms the firm's position as one of the UK's leading specialists in the field of urban light rapid transit systems. With the first trams expected to run before the end of the first decade of the 21st century the Supertram project is costing in the region of £500 million. Being built under a public/private partnership which Turner & Townsend ('T&T') had helped to finalise, and involving a likely four year construction programme, the scheme is far from being T&T's first such project. Since project managing the pioneering South Yorkshire Supertram in Sheffield, T&T has amassed a unique track record of experience in the development of new urban transport systems. T&T earlier monitored the construction of the Croydon Tramlink project and is currently

involved in major schemes in both Nottingham and Bristol.

Around Leeds, the firm of Turner and Townsend has become a familiar name, having been prominent in such projects as the remodelling of Leeds railway station and the construction of the Jubilee Building for Leeds General Infirmary. Further afield, this once small firm has been involved in much, much more, both in the UK and internationally, in the process acquiring a

*Above: Celebrating 50 years of Turner & Townsend, and former Chairman Geoff Townsend (centre), former Chairman Jeff Smith (left) and current Chairman Tim Wray. Below: The opening of the company's Newcastle office in 1960. Cornelius HA Tuner back left with his wife Joy and Geoff Townsend third from the right with wife Gloria.*

world-wide reputation. But where did this growing colossus come from?

On 1st April 1946, wartime colleagues Cornelius Turner and Francis 'Frank' Ing, two young men who had their early careers as quantity surveyors interrupted by the second world war, joined in partnership on their demobilisation and formed the quantity surveying practice of Turner & Ing.

During the last year of the war in Europe, Captain CHA Turner had met Corporal FG Ing in one of the few houses still standing in Bayeaux. Due to their difference in rank, Captain Turner was billeted in the house whilst Corporal Ing was living in a tent in the garden. Both, however were founder members of 160 CRE, the military equivalent of the County Engineers and Surveyors Department. Various postings followed Bayeaux, including a relatively long spell in Mariakerke in Belgium, during which a friendship was formed between the Captain and the Corporal; the difference in their military ranks being made far less divisive by their both being associate members of the Surveyors Institute.

In 1946 the pair opened a modest office in Darlington, shortly afterwards opening premises at Aycliffe Industrial Estate to deal with commissions from North East Trading Estates, Newton Aycliffe and Peterlee New Town.

When the practice started at the end of the war there was a huge amount of work involved in rebuilding the country after years of neglect - and the attempts of Hitler's Luftwaffe to bomb Britain into submission. Projects involving housing, heavy engineering and manufacturing were a national priority.

By the end of the 1940s the small quantity surveying firm had 15 members of staff. Geoff Townsend joined in 1949 and became a partner in 1953. He took an active part in quantity surveying's professional body, the RICS, and was eventually President of its QS division in 1979, and Institution in 1984.

Offices were opened in Durham, Teesside and Newcastle in 1953 to cope with local projects which had now become very diversified to include heavy engineering, petrochemicals and landscape works. At the close of the 1950s Prime Minster Harold Macmillan would famously announce 'You've never had it so good'. And it was true: the dereliction and neglect of the war years was over. New buildings were springing up everywhere - and in the wake of growing prosperity quantity surveyors could thrive.

***Above:*** *The Prince of Wales Colliery.*

On the departure of Frank Ing in 1956, the practice had become Turner & Townsend. In that year the firm expanded by opening offices in Leeds, Manchester, Sheffield and London, though it would not be until 1972 that the firm opened its first permanent office in Leeds at CMA House in Park Place, before eventually moving to offices at 5 Portland Street.

Having worked on projects internationally for many years, in 1982, following the award of major mining commissions, the practice opened an office in Johannesburg in the Republic of South Africa and over the following years acquired businesses in Zimbabwe, Malawi, Botswana, Zambia and Mozambique.

Getting started in South Africa was not quite as easy as one might think. In order to trade in South Africa it was necessary for a company to be registered. In 1983 Chairman Geoff Townsend went out to Johannesburg to sort out problems with the registration in person. He met the President of the Registration Council for discussions, only to be told that as the senior partner he would be required to sit an examination, and asked when he would like to take it! Not to be deterred, Geoff replied 'Now'. He was then subjected to a 50 minute oral examination by a Professor of Quantity Surveying from Pretoria

University and by the Senior Visiting Lecturer of Wits University. Geoff was mightily relieved to be told afterwards that he had passed with flying colours - despite his modest observation that he was surprised that he still knew so much about quantity surveying. Offices would subsequently be opened in Europe and the Far East, and more recently in the USA and Australia.

In 1987, a new focussed management service was offered through the practice's first separate limited company named Turner & Townsend Project Management Ltd. In future years, Turner & Townsend Facilities Management and Turner & Townsend Management Systems (later

***This page:*** *Low Hall, the company Head Office.*

renamed Turner & Townsend Management Solutions) were successfully developed out of the Project Management division. In addition, in 1994, a contract services company, Stephen Pymont & Co was bought and renamed Turner & Townsend Contract Services.

On 5th June 1995 Turner & Townsend moved from Portland Street to Low Hall in Horsforth, a location which now became the whole Group's head office after the closure of its Darlington premises.

The first mention of Low Hall appears in 1565 when John Stanhope, himself a descendant of Sir Richard Stanhope the owner of large estates in Northumberland in the reign of Henry III and Edward I, moved to Horsforth to become part-purchaser of the Monastery of Kirkstall and a one fourth purchaser of the Manor of Horsforth. He took up residence in Low Hall, where four generations of his family lived until 1699 when John Stanhope, who had succeeded to the estate at the age of just 16 in 1694, built Horsforth Hall whilst Low Hall continued to be occupied by his relatives.

The present Low Hall was built some 150 years after the original building circa 1710. The entrance and north wing were added at an unknown later date and the two halls joined together. The buildings were then separated once more in the early years of the 20th century. Low Hall remained in the ownership of the Stanhope family for over 400 years until 1972 when it was bought by the Greenwood family and converted into a well known restaurant prior to its acquisition by the T&T Group in 1995.

In 2000, the T&T Group acquired Pace Project Services, a specialist division with expertise in the oil, gas and heavy engineering industries. The following year the Group formed a joint venture company with Siemens - Siemens Industrial Building Consultants (SIBC) which offered consultancy services for hi-tech projects: things had changed remarkably in the course of more than half a century, and yet throughout that period continuity had also played a strong part.

Jeff Smith joined Turner & Ing in 1955 and went on to become Chairman of the Turner & Townsend Group in 1992 before retiring in 1999. Tim Wray, Group Chairman at the start of the 21st century, joined in 1971 and having worked in the Leeds and Wakefield offices became the major figure in developing the practice in Africa before returning to

*Below:* Nissan Motor Manufacturing (UK)Limited. Ground breaking in Washington 1983. T&T have a long term relationship with Nissan and now work with them in Europe and the USA. Pictured from second left are: Tom Harrison (now MD of T&T International), A Shimanuki, Nissan (head of engineering), Roger Lush, T&T, Geoff Townsend, T&T, Wes Molyneux, T&T, and David Barry, T&T.

Britain in 1999 to take overall responsibility for the Group.

Alistair Wilson joined in 1977 and became a partner in 1986; he started Turner & Townsend Project Management in 1987 on behalf of the partnership and would become Managing Director of Turner & Townsend UK. Tom Harrison also joined the practice in 1977, becoming a partner in 1990 before becoming Managing Director of Turner & Townsend International.

Following in Geoff Townsend's footsteps, his son Paul joined the practice as a Quantity Surveyor. Paul continued a close association with academia and was especially interested in the development of computing systems within the industry. Paul would eventually leave T&T to pursue a career in academia.

Though Paul may have left, his brother, Nick would continue the Townsend family connection. Nick Townsend joined in 1988 - initially via an industrial experience placement as a student in Newcastle. He became a partner in 1995 and was based in Newcastle before relocating to Leeds in 1995 and subsequently running the Cost Management Division for the Leeds region. Today Turner & Townsend is no longer a 'family firm' but an international corporate partnership.

Not that Turner & Townsend is, or ever has been, behind the times in its attitudes and practices - it has the reputation for being one of the most innovative and forward looking firms in the industry: it was one of the first to introduce computers and fax machines to its offices in the UK and was at the forefront of developing disciplines such as Project Management, Risk and Value Management and Cost Engineering. The last three decades or so have seen

the decline of many traditional industries in the UK, particularly mining, heavy engineering and manufacturing - Turner & Townsend's main markets in the early years. Today the firm's market is far more diverse and covers both public and private sectors: within the UK the firm is heavily involved in the public sector in health, education and transport. The private sector covers a wide range of commissions such as shops, offices, telecommunications and transport.

In the 1990s, Turner & Townsend was involved in more than 50 urban regeneration projects in the UK alone, projects with a combined value well in excess of £2 billion. Those projects ranged from small, highly localised housing developments to the revitalisation of complete city areas such as Glasgow's £150 million Crown Street Project, Elephant and Castle regeneration in London and the 'Liverpool Vision'.

T&T was also closely involved in rebuilding Manchester's shattered city centre following the IRA bombing, whilst abroad the Group would be actively involved in advising the Italian Government on a major programme of urban regener-

*Above:* The redevelopment of Leeds Station.
**Below, both pictures:** *Two of T&T's projects, the Yorkshire Bank (left) and The Leeds Permanent Building Society Headquarters a T&T project from 1988-1993.*

Metro Extension, Milan its Museum of 20th Century Art and the Netherlands its SAS Hotel; the Americas have their Nissan North American Retail Roll Out, whilst Asia has seen new Siemens offices in Singapore and Beijing.

What next for this award winning firm? By 2002 it had more than 1000 staff representing 14 different professional disciplines based in a worldwide network of offices. Tim Wray's plans for the future are clear: to

ation affecting 50 key brown field sites throughout that country.

Overseas, however, heavy engineering and mining still continue to form a large part of the firm's commissions. These markets are complemented by newer sectors such as microelectronics and tourism.

Over the years Turner and Townsend has made a remarkable contribution to major projects across the whole of the United Kingdom, making critical contributions to schemes such as the Heathrow Express and Terminal 5, the Tate Gallery, the Imperial War Museum North, the headquarters of the Greater London Assembly, the Welcome Trust HQ and the Glasgow Science Centre amongst many others. Overseas every continent has benefited from the contribution of Turner and Townsend. Africa has its University of Bulawayo and its De Beers headquarters; in Europe, Rome has its

continue to grow the business, to reach out for new challenges and ensure that the Group becomes even more robust whilst maintaining its head office, and the hub of its world-wide operations, at Low Hall in Leeds.

*Top left:* The stunning Manchester Imperial War Museum on which Turner & Townsend provided full Commercial Management service for the base build project and also helped value engineer the initial concepts into a more affordable proposal in order to make the project possible.
*Above left:* After a highly competitive bid process, T&T won the commission to serve as both Project and Cost Managers on one of the largest new office developments to take place in Cape Town in the last 10 years.
*Below left:* City Hall, the new headquarters for the Greater London Authority. *Below:* The Leeds General Infirmary, a project of the company from 1997-2001.

# *The hippest firm in town*

When, in April 1990, Boehringer Mannheim bought up Leeds' Charles F Thackray Ltd it acquired a world-famous company with a history almost as long as its own. That change led to a new name for 'Thackray's': DePuy International.

The Thackray acquisition brought together two of the world's leading manufacturers of total hip replacements. Thackray was also known for providing healthcare services to British consumers through its Thackray-Care centres.

Thackray's origins were remarkably similar to those of Boehringer Mannheim's DePuy company: for example both Charles F Thackray and DePuy's

founder, Revra DePuy had a pharmaceutical background. Having trained as a pharmacist in England and gained further experience working in London, and also in both France and Switzerland, in 1902, at the age of 25, Charles Thackray had bought the pharmacy of Samuel Taylor in Leeds, a business which had already been in existence since 1862.

supplies, and also as an important wholesaler and manufacture of pharmaceuticals and dressings. The adoption by the War Office of the Thackray 'Aseptic' dressing as a standard field dressing resulted in the rapid expansion of the company during the Great War.

After the war's end the company continued to enjoy rapid growth, with the emphasis now changing from pharmaceuticals and dressings to the manufacture and distribution of surgical instruments and equipment. The level of expansion is illustrated by the fact that in 1925 the company began exporting products to British Empire markets including Canada, Australia and South Africa. Charles Thackray died in 1934 and his two sons, C Noel and WP 'Tod' Thackray, became directors of the commercial manufacturing operation.

In 1940, in the early stages of the second world war, the company's product range expanded once again, this time to include sterilisers, operating tables, patient-handling equipment and electro-surgical equipment. During the war

Between 1906 and 1908 Thackray diversified from retail pharmacy into making quality surgical instruments. His company also established a contract sterilising service for local nursing homes and hospitals. On the outbreak of the first world war in 1914 Thackray was recognised throughout the north of England as a reliable distributor of a broad range of surgical

***Above***: *Thackray's original premises.*
***Right***: *Thackray's staff line-up for a photocall in the late 1970s.*

established the gold standard of artificial total hip replacements, or prosthetics, known simply as 'The Charnley'.

The first instruments which Thackray's made for John Charnley in 1947 were devices used to insert the guidewires used in pinning femoral neck fractures.

After 1963 Charnley would specialise almost exclusively in hip surgery and worked closely with Arthur Hallam, a foreman in Thackray's development workshop who was involved in every detail of the development of 'low friction arthoplasty'.

Thackray's began making Charnley's high molecular weight polyethylene acetabular sockets in 1963. Charnley originally manufactured the sockets himself. Thackray's however manufactured Charnley's femoral components from the beginning; for every prosthetic sold the company contributed one pound to the research fund at the Wrightington Hospital, near Wigan, where Charnley would establish the Centre of Excellence for Total Hip Replacement. Charnley wrote almost every week to Thackray's offering suggestions, criticisms and compliments such as 'I am quite sure that the defective workmanship would not have occurred in the days of Mr Hallam' and 'The femoral punch is an excellent job'. In 1968 alone Charnley wrote 46 letters to Thackray employees.

years the company also pioneered the development of instrumentation for skin grafting and plastic surgery.

The company's interest in orthopaedics began in 1947 when it began to manufacture a variety of orthopaedic instruments. In 1950 Thackray's was approached by a surgeon working in Manchester who required an instrument to assist in the fixation and treatment of femoral neck fractures - breaks in the hip bone where it meets the pelvis. That approach was to change not only the destiny of Thackray's but also set the standard for present day total hip replacements. The surgeon was Sir John Charnley who, together with Thackray's,

*Top left: A manufacturing area at Thackrays.*
*Above and right: Two operating tables, manufactured by the firm for Airedale Hospital .*

In the early 1970s Tod Thackray became chairman and managing director of Thackray's; his son John P Thackray became deputy managing director whilst his nephew C Paul Thackray became a director.

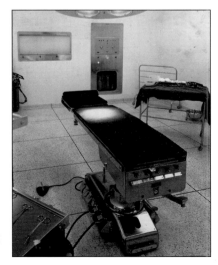

By 1971 Thackray's was manufacturing up to 10,000 'stems' a year - Charnley however thought it should be producing 100,000!

John Charnley helped raise standards and remained loyal to the company throughout his career, though once writing 'In Britain it is not considered good form to acknowledge commercial undertakings in too glowing terms, even though the work would not have been possible without their collaboration...'

In the 1970s a problem both Charnley and Thackray's faced was the abundance of imitations of his prosthesis. The stem was widely copied both because it was never patented, and also because a good product will always be imitated. Another problem they faced was other companies using the Charnley name. In one case, the 'Charnley-Muller' prosthesis, John Charnley had even given his good friend Professor Maurice Muller permission to use his name. Unfortunately for Thackray's, in the USA, this stem became the surgeon's prosthesis of choice.

Despite such worries no area of detail remained too small for Charnley to take an interest in. His last letter to the company, dated 8th July 1982, concerned the description of his prostheses and instruments as they would appear in Thackray's new catalogue. The catalogue was not printed until after Charnley's unexpected death on 5th August 1982. In the introduction to the catalogue Tod Thackray wrote 'Chas F Thackray and myself in particular feel honoured that we were allowed to participate in the development and

manufacture of his instruments and prostheses, used and proven by Sir John in the 26 years applied to the perfection of his very

successful operation. Perhaps only once in a lifetime does one come across a man prepared to devote so much time in one direction...'

In the 1980s, with Tod Thackray still at the helm, the company was restructured into six divisions: Orthopaedics, Orthogenesis, ThackrayCare, Surgery, Pearce Laboratories and VetBed. At that time Thackray's was the market leader in the United Kingdom in replacement joints and had sales staff and distributorships in 100 countries. The company accounted for 18 per cent of all the replacement joints sold in the world outside of the USA.

Tod Thackray was still chairman in 1990 at the time the company was bought by Boehringer Mannheim, Europe's largest pharmaceutical company; he died in 1993. The new owners also owned the American orthopaedics company DePuy. When John Thackray retired Buck Keeney became president of DePuy's

*Top left*: A manufacturing area at Thackray's.
*Top right:* On-going training at Thackray's.
*Above right:* An employee receiving a Thackray apprentice award. *Left:* Manufacturing area at Thackrays.

international operations after being vice president of finance at DePuy.

Intriguingly DePuy was the company which had acquired the marketing rights to Maurice Muller's prosthesis in the 1960s. That event had changed the DePuy company's image from that of a soft goods company selling mainly rib belts, collars, braces and some pins and wires to a contender in what was then the fledgling implant market.

The DePuy company (pronounced di-pew) was an American business founded in 1895 by Revra DePuy in the small town of Warsaw, Michigan. Revra DePuy had been a travelling pharmaceutical salesman before establishing his then small factory which made fibre splints for doctors to use when setting broken limbs. Remarkably one of DePuy's earliest employees was a young Justin O Zimmer whose own company, set up in 1927, would itself become an equally famous name. By the time of his death in 1921

Revra DePuy had become one of Warsaw's most prominent businessmen. He left behind him a widow, Winifred, who, alongside her second and considerably younger second husband Herschel Leiter, would run the company until 1949. Winifred DePuy had died in May 1949 and the widowed Herschel remarried the following November only to die himself six months later from a heart attack. Thirteen months later Herschel's widow Amrette married a Bell-Telephone executive named Harry Hoopes, though it was Amrette who now ran the company.

In 1965 the Hoopes sold the still small but profitable company to investors for $1.3 million. Three years later the company was sold on to Bio-Dynamics a blood diagnostic business for more than $3 million. That same year the company acquired rights to the Muller artificial hip and, with increased investment, the company now began to grow, continuing to do so after Bio-Dynamics was itself acquired by Boehringer in 1974.

In November 1991, some 18 months after Thackray's was itself acquired by Boehringer Mannheim Thackray's was renamed as DePuy International Ltd and Bill Todmore was named President. The perfect fit between the two original companies' product lines and manufacturing techniques was the reason cited for establishing DePuy's international headquarters, as well as its European manufacturing plant, in Leeds. Work had begun earlier that year to create DePuy's international headquarters, and to further invest in a new modern plant, at the Leeds site. The new international headquarters were officially opened by Herr Professor Helmut Determann, Boehringer Mannheim's Chief Executive.

*Top right*: *Manufacturing areas.* **Above left:** *A manufacturing area at Thackrays.* **Left:** *A roll call of staff who've received an apprenticeship award.*

The official ribbon-cutting ceremony for the new building was attended by Lady Charnley who continued to have contact with DePuy International and be actively involved in the administration of the Charnley Trust, a foundation used to financially assist surgeons with their continuing education and training.

When Johnson & Johnson purchased DePuy in November 1998 the result was a merger of companies with a combined total of over 300 years experience in the application of science and engineering in the field of medicine.

Johnson & Johnson traced its origins to 1886 when Robert Wood Johnson and his two brothers founded a medical products company in New Brunswick, New Jersey. It was good time to set up a business: with the Civil War long over America was in a buoyant mood. There was an avalanche of ideas to feed the population's insatiable appetite for all things new. And high on the nation's list of priorities were products to promote better health.

At the same time, internationally, there were rapid advances in medicine; one of the most fundamental being the work of Joseph Lister in Britain who put into practice Pasteur's theory that germs caused infection. Inspired by Lister's work on antiseptics Robert Johnson grasped the potential for sterile aseptic surgical dressings; the company developed the bandages and other dressings which were to establish its reputation. There followed a continuous stream of other surgical products and medicines reinforcing the company's reputation for innovation and integrity which would become its hallmark.

Of the galaxy of Johnson & Johnson's household brand names one of the most outstanding would be the Band-Aid adhesive bandage, invented in 1920, and becoming the biggest seller in the company's history. But no product would do more for its corporate image than Johnson's Baby Powder upon which the company would build a vast business for nursery items.

The J&J operation outside North America began in the United Kingdom in 1924 when a plant was opened in Slough. More companies were formed in the 1930s in South Africa, Mexico, Australia, Brazil and Argentina, a process which would evolve into the vast global operation of the 21st century.

Within the UK in the 1990s DePuy had developed an unassailable reputation for providing quality products. In 1994 a number of mergers and acquisitions had established DePuy UK as a complete orthopaedic

**Top right:** *Manufacturing sterilising machines.*
**Left:** *The original Thackray site at Beeston in Leeds.*

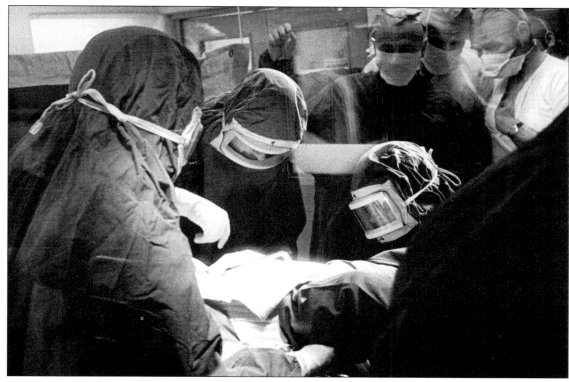

business philosophy reminds all its employees of the company's moral responsibility for all its 'constituencies': first to its customers - doctors, nurses, mothers and fathers; second to all employees who are responsible for creating the company's products; third to the communities that are affected by the company's activities and finally to its shareholders who have invested their financial resources in the company's future.

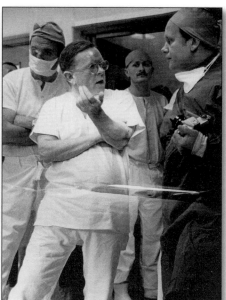

company. The addition of CMW, a manufacturer of bone cement, brought to a natural conclusion a process that had begun 30 years earlier when John Charnley had become the first orthopaedic surgeon to use the dental acrylic cement to fix an implant into bone.

Meanwhile as Johnson & Johnson had expanded, a subsidiary, Johnson & Johnson Professional, had taken on the role of promoting orthopaedic implants in 1982 when the company acquired an engineering company based in Lymington. With the development of the 'PFC knee' Johnson & Johnson became the market leader in the total knee joint market through its reputation for excellent customer service.

Written in the 1940s by Robert Wood Johnson, the son of one of the founders, the Johnson & Johnson 'Credo' or

Today many people have good reason to remember Thackray's, DePuy and Johnson & Johnson (the premiere healthcare company in the world); but the ultimate tribute to these companies and their employees however is surely the experience of the hundreds of thousands of people whose lives have been immeasurably enhanced by products made by their artisans and technicians over so many years.

*Top left and left*: *A hip operation underway by the inventor of the artificial hip, Sir John Charnley.*
*Below*: *Lady Charnley at DePuy.*

# A *fund in need*

For many folk illness is not simply an inconvenience but a cause of serious financial hardship. Even today, with the NHS proving only a basic service, there is a serious need for service and support beyond that available from the state. In the 21st century, for a small subscription, Leeds folk, and people from much further afield, can insure themselves and their dependents against mishap and misfortune with The LHF Healthplan and get both financial assistance and more direct help.

And if such a service is in high demand today how much more was such a scheme needed in the past. In 1887 Mr Fred Spark JP founded the Leeds & District Workpeoples' Hospital Fund. He determined to approach everyone in the workshops of Leeds and obtain from them weekly subscrip-

tions; that voluntary subscription was 1d per week and in the first year raised £1,883. Hospitals relied on donations for their continued existence and the Fund's purpose was to help finance local hospitals, chiefly Leeds General Infirmary, for the benefit of workers. Mr Walter Wormald was appointed the Fund's first Assistant Secretary and office premises were found at 3 Park Square after a brief period working from a single room at Peacock Buildings in Park Row.

The income of the Fund increased steadily to £13,226 by 1913. That year saw the inauguration of the compulsory National Insurance scheme introduced by Chancellor Lloyd George for workers which provided unemployment benefit and 'free' primary care for insured workers. This could have had serious repercussions but fortunately by that time the Fund was too well established and in any event the 1913 legislation was limited in its scope. Chairman Fred Spark reported at the Annual General meeting that when they

*Above left*: Founder, Fred Spark.
*Below:* The executive committee from 1900 with Fred Spark seated centre with his wife.

came to consider that the working men of Leeds had to pay a compulsory 4d per week out of their income and in addition were voluntarily giving 1d per week to the Fund it must be agreed by all that it was a very creditable effort. He added that he thought the 1d per week paid to the Fund was worth more to the man in personal benefit than the 4d per week with which he was taxed.

By the early 1930s the Fund had become a more formalised 'contributory scheme', with the, now 2d per week, subscriptions collected systematically and the end of casual collections and fund-raising for individual hospitals. Membership of the Fund had grown to 150,000 with most of the money collected being disbursed to hospitals. In addition to workers' contributions several other methods of raising monies for medical charities were employed.

Many older readers from around Leeds will still recall the Annual Hospital Galas held in Roundhay Park on Bank Holidays. The prizes on offer to winners of the various events brought together some of the best athletes in the country; there were concerts, brass bands, gymnastic displays, Punch and Judy shows and fireworks displays. One year the Gala featured a circus whilst on another occasion a hot air balloon ascent was the highlight of the day.

Attendance at the first Gala in 1887 was 22,000, and of such interest was the event that over 3,000 people were brought into Leeds for it by excursion trains. The last such Gala would be held on the eve of war in 1939.

Just before the war, in 1937, the Fund marked its Golden Jubilee by making a special £1,000 gift to Leeds General Infirmary for the dedication of a new ward to be named after the Fund.

The war years of 1939-45 saw the gestation of today's NHS. The start of the Welfare State and the National Health

*Top: A slightly later picture of the committee Fred Spark can be seen in the centre with an umbrella. Left: Burlington Convalescent Home for Men, opened in June 1949. Below: The Dinning Room at Burlington.*

Service in July 1948 led to a depressing fall in income for the Fund. Contributory Schemes in many other towns and cities ceased to operate, but not so in Leeds. Behind the facade of No 3 Park Square, a revised scheme was drawn up offering to members, their non-working wives and dependent children direct benefits which would go beyond the services offered by the NHS. Many subscribers withdrew their membership but thousands decided, like the Fund, to carry on being conscious from the outset that many desirable features of a health service were not going to be provided by the NHS - a situation which would be underscored in 1951 when NHS charges were introduced for prescriptions, dental services and glasses.

With the inauguration of the NHS, after allowing for substantial year end disbursements, the balance of monies was needed to create the foundation of the new scheme. Reserves were created to meet the cost of claims for the first year, particularly the Hospital In-patient Cash Grant, the cost of which for the first year was estimated to be £30,000 - and astonishingly proved to be correct to within £250. A General Reserve was also created to meet any unforeseeable emergency such as unemployment. The whole structure of the Fund as it was prior to 1948 was drastically changed, and it now became a movement which, by the systematic collection of small regular amounts from subscribers, was able to supplement the benefits of the NHS and 'help maintain in some measure that freedom of choice which is so characteristic of the British'.

The Fund responded with a scheme that would provide supplementary benefits to the subscriber whilst the income from the Reserve Fund was made available for several charitable disbursements. The ethos of the scheme has remained the same ever since.

The popularity of the Revised Scheme and the increased number of callers at the Fund's offices now made it apparent that the premises in Park Square were no longer adequate to house the number of staff needed to deal with increased business. At the time office accommodation was at a premium, whilst obtaining a Building Licence in that period of post war austerity and rationing was anything but easy. Premises at 41 St Paul's Street were however

*Above: One of the Leeds Hospital Fund's buses taking convalescent patients to Ilkley. Below left: The official opening of the Manor Convalescent Home, 1953. Below: The opening of St Pauls Street by the Lord Mayor, 1955.*

ence for going to the coast for their convalescence.

Accordingly 1949 saw the opening of the Fund's first seaside convalescent home. A property then known as the Burlington Hotel, in Bridlington was bought and adapted for use as a men's home. This quickly proved so popular that it was decided to provide a similar seaside home for women. Always bearing in mind the question of transport the Fund now purchased another property in Bridlington, The Manor Hotel. The conversion of that building was on an extensive scale, and as with the new offices the licensing position was difficult; in fact so restricted were building licences at that time that the Fund had to choose between the new home or the new office premises. The needs of convalescent patients won the day and plans went ahead. The new home was opened in September 1953 by the Rt Hon The Viscountess Swinton

It was not until 1955 that the Fund's offices moved to 41 St Paul's Street after 68 years at premises in Park Square.

The two homes in Bridlington continued to operate well for the next 20 years until in 1969 a major decision was made to build a new purpose built home to improve the facilities offered to patients.

purchased in 1950 for £6,850. The purchase was however only a first step, and in the ensuing years the Fund's architects proceeded to convert the building for its new role, reducing it to a shell before reconstructing it throughout.

Meanwhile other major building work was afoot. Benefits provided by the Fund had not just consisted of money and improved hospital facilities.

Since 1896 convalescence has played an important part in the work of the Fund. The first Home owned and operated by the Fund was 'Springfield' at Horsforth which was opened by the then Lord Mayor of Leeds, Alderman CF Tetley. More than 500 people attended the opening ceremony after being ferried in a cavalcade of wagonettes from Leeds Town Hall to Horsforth in the rain.

That first convalescent home proved to be so popular that others were acquired locally, equipped and staffed, though they would later be disposed of, as and when they became redundant, in a response to members expressing a prefer-

*Above:* Viewing of some of the equipment donated to local hospitals. *Above left:* A selection of Leeds Hospital Fund trophies. *Below:* The opening of the headquarters in November 1955 by the Lord Mayor of Leeds, Sir James Croysdale.

District Workpeoples Hospital Fund to the Leeds and District Hospital Fund. Just 11 years later the name would change again as interest in the Fund increased far beyond the immediate vicinity of Leeds; the words 'and District' were now deleted and at the same time legal steps were taken to change the name of the Fund to the Leeds Hospital fund Ltd.

By the year 2000 the office premises at 41 St Paul's street where the Leeds Hospital Fund Ltd had spent 45 years had become inadequate and it was necessary to move to larger premises at Canal Wharf. The new office was built to the specific requirements of LHF and would be the base for some 50 employees with enough room for further growth.

In the millennium year the Leeds Hospital Fund Charitable Trust made its largest single donation ever, providing a sum of £500,000 towards the Millennium Project. That funding enabled Leeds General Infirmary to create a Children's Unit and a Children's Neuroscience Unit.

The Trustees felt it appropriate to look to fund a specific project to mark the Millennium, and the consensus was

Demolition of the property known originally as the Burlington and which had subsequently been renamed Springfield now took place and a new Springfield was opened by the Lord Mayor of Leeds, Alderman Trevor Watson, in September 1971. The new home was planned to accommodate both male and female patients whilst the Manor, being now surplus to requirements, was sold by auction in 1972.

The years between 1971 and 1985 saw great social change in the holiday habits of contributors. Many were spending their holidays abroad and, if staying in this country, the standard expected of hotels by them became much higher. That change had an adverse effect on the number and age group of contributors applying for convalescence. The original concept of the Fund's home had been to provide recuperative convalescence so workers could benefit from a stay at a home before returning to work. This was not happening, so several alterations were made in an attempt to attract the worker who had been ill and would benefit from a stay at Springfield. The following year many of the old fashioned rules at the home were relaxed and room facilities upgraded, for example by enabling patients to make tea or coffee in their rooms. A bar was also provided where patients could drink and enjoy a relaxed atmosphere providing more of a real hotel feel to Springfield.

In 1970 the name of the Fund had been formally changed from the Leeds and

*Top left*: One of the many Leeds Hospital Fund vans providing chiropody services. ***Above right***: The Executive Committee, 1980. ***Right***: Springfield Convalescent Home, Bridlington, opened in 1971 by Alderman and Lord Mayor of Leeds, Trevor Watson.

May 2002 saw the retirement of LHF's Chief Executive, Angela Romaine, who had worked for the Fund for 39 years, the new Managing Director became Lysanne McCallion.

In the following months LHF would launch a new revised scheme, now costing just £2.49 per week, still offering all the old favourites like dental, optical and physiotherapy but also including such modern day services such as health screening in addition to many other benefits such as a stay at the Springfield convalescent home.

In the future the LHF aims to continue providing an efficient, not for profit service, which turns subscriber's claims around quickly and provides high returns on benefits with the main focus of attention always being the subscriber.

that such a project should look towards the future of the community - there is no better way to mark the future than by helping the next generation, our children.

Overall the Leeds Hospital Fund Charitable Trust donated around one million pounds in 2001 to many worthy causes including hospices, hospitals and other health related charities including the funding of the Leeds Hospital Fund Convalescent Home in Bridlington.

Early in 2002 LHF merged with HSA one of the UK's leading 'cash plan' providers. Together the two organisations would have over a million subscribers and an annual income of some £163 million.

Computerisation had begun in 1982 to help run the accounts of the 52,000 out of 200,000 subscribers who paid directly into the Fund. By 2002 the whole system would be computerised helping LHF to deal with the 1,800 claims it was by now receiving each and every day.

Today it is almost impossible to calculate just how many Leeds folk have benefited from subscribing to this remarkable body which was founded in the late 19th century on a wave of enthusiasm for self help. That any organisation should survive for so long, and continue to prosper, remains an enduring tribute to its farsighted founder Fred Spark.

*Top left*: The presentation of the Millennium Project Donation. *Above*: Launched in July 2002, a LHF Health booklet showing current benefits on offer. *Below left*: Lysanne McCallion, Managing Director. *Below*: Current premises at Canal Wharf.

# A printer's tale

What does the name Jowett & Sowry mean to you? Come to that what did it mean to your parents and grandparents? They would certainly all have recognised the name of this long established Leeds-based stationery and office supplies company which has been in business in the city since the later years of Queen Victoria's reign.

In September 1888, the year after the Queen's Golden Jubilee, the founders of what would become Jowett & Sowry Ltd, Charles Jowett and John Percy Sowry (known as J.P.), left their jobs as compositors with a large printing firm and started their own printing business in part of a building in 73 Albion Street Leeds which was then being used as a china warehouse. In those days Albion Street was a backwater, its upper end leading to Upperhead Row, where the Headrow is today, being then not much more than a passageway. From the start the new business prospered and quite soon additional space was taken for the growing printing business whilst the partners also opened a shop for selling stationery and paper. By 1883 a manager and two apprentices were employed in the shop.

In 1891 the founders were joined in partnership by Henry Armitage and the business moved to larger premises on the opposite side of Albion Street where lithography and bookbinding were added to the letterpress side of the business.

By 1904, from its tiny beginnings, the firm of Jowett & Sowry could boast on its letterhead of being art catalogue printers, chromo lithographers, folding box manufacturers, book binders, stationers and account book manufacturers as well as having substantial premises not only in Albion Street but in Park Row and a branch in Halifax, as well as occupying the Electric Printing Works in Balm Road, Hunslet.

Charles Jowett died in 1917 and was buried at Roundhay. Despite that loss the business continued to grow and eventually the whole building in Albion Street, extending back to King Charles Street, was occupied; in addition an extension covering an open yard facing on to Albion Street was built in 1929.

*Above: Co-founder John Percy Sowry.*
*Below: A company letterhead from 1904.*

By now J.P. Sowry had become chairman of what was a limited company rather than a partnership: the business having been incorporated in 1918 with himself, Henry Armitage, HS Wainwright and George W Wilkinson as its directors. It would however still be lonely at the top: Henry Armitage had died in 1925 and was buried at Lawnswood, tragically both he and J.P. Sowry had each lost their only sons as a consequence of the first world war. J.P.'s son Lieutenant Alfred Allan Sowry had been killed in action in France, Henry Armitage's son had however not succumbed to his injuries until 1925, remarkably dying on the same day as his father.

Despite those tragedies business continued. In the 1930s, with the extension four storeys high, the premises were extensive and included three shops, each with separate entrances, selling stationery, art and drawing office materials and office furniture. Office furniture was first sold as a joint venture with a firm of steel furniture makers Sankey-Sheldon Ltd. Ever since the business had begun the printing works had been the dominant side of the firm, producing large amounts of printed materials for Leeds Corporation, Leeds University and for commercial and industrial concerns mainly in Yorkshire but also for London and the south-east. However the retail side had not been neglected and by the thirties there were branches of the firm in Halifax, Manchester and Doncaster.

Any further development had however to be deferred following the outbreak of war with Nazi Germany in 1939. During the war years of 1939-45 the company did its bit by being involved in producing printed material for government departments and anti-radar material for the RAF.

***Top:*** *Printing in the mid 20th century.*
***Above left****: The company premises pictured in 1961.*

some premises almost opposite the original site became available and the shop moved across the road ensuring that the business would in due course eventually be able to celebrate its centenary in Albion Street. From 1962 the Albion Street stationery business developed gradually, slowly concentrating more on office supplies, writing instruments and art materials whilst reducing the household stationery lines which were stocked. Moving into its heyday in the 1970s, from having been a two man partnership at its outset, the company by now employed some 85 staff.

In the 1980s the company's centenary in Albion Street would be celebrated by a major refurbishment which involved a new shopfront and facia. Improved interior lighting and display units enabled the company to provide customers with a wide choice of all types of art materials, technical drawing equipment and stationery which by now included computer supplies.

Throughout these long years the company remained independent. By now its Chairman and Managing Director was Michael Sowry Sheard the grandson of J.P. Sowry who had remained active in the business until his death in 1959 at the age of 91. Michael Sheard joined the company when he was 15 and succeeded his grandfather in 1959 as chairman.

The next generation of the family was to be represented by Michael's son, Jonathan Sheard, who was at first involved in the sale of office furniture at Armley Road, officially working

After the war, though all materials were in short supply, the company gradually returned to normal. The arrangement with Sankey-Sheldon had ended with the war and from then on furniture was bought independently from several manufacturers. In 1952 the office furniture department was transferred to larger premises in King Street where bigger displays were possible. The growth of the furniture side of the business coupled with the difficulties of storing and transporting furniture in the city centre prompted a further move in 1969 to a former engineering works at 164 Armley Road which is still the main showroom and warehouse for office furniture and commercial stationery and which would also house the company head office with its computerised accounting facilities for the whole group. The printing works was moved to modern premises in York Road in 1962 where it would remain until 1972 when it was sold to another Yorkshire printer, Watmoughs Holdings plc with Jowett & Sowry returning ownership of the property on York Road. During the 1960s the different businesses operated entirely separately as Jowett & Sowry (Printers) Ltd and Jowett & Sowry (Office Supplies) Ltd until the printing business became Jowetts (Printers) Ltd when it was sold whilst the office supplies business reverted to the original and shorter name Jowett & Sowry Ltd.

*Above left:* Albion Street, 1963.
*Below:* The modern printworks on York Road which Jowett & Sowry used until 1972 before selling the print business to Watmoughs Holdings plc.

Meanwhile, when the printing works had moved in 1962, the premises in Albion Street were sold for redevelopment and consequently the shop had to move. Fortunately

Jowett & Sowry Office Design from Armley Road.

Despite being more than 100 years old the company has always kept up to date with current technology and customers' requirements. The changes from hand written ledgers to machine accounting, then to computerised ledgers and finally to a fully integrated order and stocking system have required considerable training and staff involvement and the company now has a large training facility to ensure that staff and customers can equally be kept abreast of the latest developments such as computer aided design (CAD) and office design and layout.

for Planned Offices Ltd, a wholly owned subsidiary of Jowett & Sowry, which provided an interior design and planning service for offices and business suites. By the 1980s, in addition to office furniture, the Albion Street building also housed the company's huge stock of commercial stationery supplied direct to professional, commercial and industrial users as well as to the shops in Albion Street and to the company's branches which now existed in Halifax, Doncaster and Selby.

At the start of the 21st century the company still remains a private, family owned firm, its chairman is JP Sowry's great grandson, Jonathan David Sowry Sheard. Jonathan, representing the fourth generation of his family, had been made MD in 1992, having previously been joint Managing Director with former Company Secretary Brian Sharp since 1990.

Having been founded in the 19th century now, in the 21st century, the flair, innovation and enthusiasm which first drove the firm's founders continued to enthuse their successors - as a result, four generations of the company's customers, the name of Jowett & Sowry has been and remains synonymous with quality, service and customer satisfaction.

*Top left:* Mrs Margery Mitchell is presented with a retirement gift by the chairman Michael Sowry Sheard. Mrs Mitchell joined Jowett & Sowry as a young girl and after marriage and having a family returned to the company until her retirement in 1980. *Below:* Jowett & Sowry's premises on Armley Road in 2002.

In a further round of change the company sold its commercial stationery business to Dales Stationery Supplies in 2001 but retained the retail shop in the Headrow.

Gilly Sheard, Jonathan's sister, who had been working for the office furniture division for some eight years now became a director following which Jonathan and Gilly now jointly run

# More light - and heat

Today more than 150 employees work at Bray Burners Ltd, the Leeds-based gas engineering firm. But the company has employed many thousands of Leeds folk over the course of its long existence.

The business founded in 1863 by George Bray, who after becoming a printer's devil at the age of 11 devoted his evenings to classes at the Leeds Mechanics Institute. A reference at a lecture on gas lighting to the inadequacy of the iron gas burners used in those days gave the young George the idea of improving them to produce a better gas light.

George's aim was to produce a gas burner with a porcelain tip which would resist the corrosion which affected iron burners and was caused by impurities in the gas. Experiments conducted in the attic of his parents' house so frightened his family that he rented a small workshop.

Working in the middle of the night, and having burnt all the available fuel when close to success, he rushed to his parents' house and took away enough furniture to stoke his furnace. One only hopes that his parents forgave him when the end result of his labours, and their sacrifice, was George's first patent.

For a century, from 1863 when George Bray made his first ceramic tipped jet, to 1963 when the first aerated burners were produced the company held a dominant position as a

*Above: An engraving of Bray Burners premises from the early 1900s. Left: Company founder George Bray. Below: An exhibition stand from the late 1800s.*

supplier of non-aerated jets to the gas industry.

A non-aerated jet consisted of a ceramic tip with an appropriately shaped orifice mounted on a metal socket provided with a means of attachment to a gas supply. Gas was mixed with air as it emerged from the orifice after the point of combustion. In this respect it differed from an aerated burner where air is mixed with gas before the point of combustion. Such a jet is only suitable for use with fast burning gasses such as acetylene or coal gas, whereas aerated burners can be used with any gas including natural gas and liquid petroleum gas.
By the early 1870s the firm was based in a factory in

*Top: An exhibition from the 1950s.*
*Above left: Demolition of the old works in 1973.*

Blackman Lane, but as the business expanded it took the Lamp Works at Jowett Lane where gas lamp jets would be made for bandstands, arcades and factories - and even for the London docks. The business moved to Bagby Works in Leicester Place in 1894; the new factory was situated on a large undeveloped site near Leeds University. By now Bray's 'Union Jets', 'Batswings' and 'Fishtails' with their non-corrosive porcelain tips had made George Bray famous.

In the last three decades of the 19th century patent after patent would be taken out for improving gas burners, street lamps, anti-pulsators and governors as well as for lighting, heating and ventilation. In the late 1870s George Bray introduced a new type of draught-proof street lamp with a reflector shade to avoid casting a shadow beneath it.

Gas lighting made a great leap forward in 1887 when Austrian Dr Carl Welsbach demonstrated his incandescent lamp. Bray was quick to recognise its potential and develop a new range of lights. George was however a little less clever when asked for help by Joseph Swan, the co-inventor of the electric light bulb: George told him it would never catch on.

But the Swan episode was an exception. George Bray did not miss many opportunities. Where mains gas was not available - houses in the countryside, on cars, motorcycles and bicycles the alternative was acetylene gas lighting. By 1900 leading manufacturers such as Lucas and Ford were offering Bray's burners in their products. George was also appointed to the Headingley-cum-Burley Burial Board in anticipation of the passing of the Cremation Act in 1902. With George's support Lawnswood became the first gas-fired crematorium in the country when all the others were coal or coke fired. Sadly however, due to technical difficulties, the burners had to be supplied by a French firm.

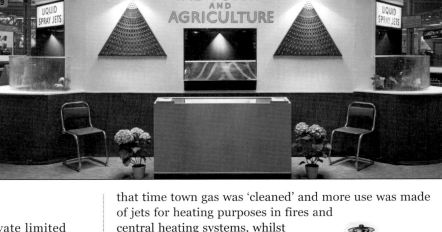

In 1903 George Bray & Co became a private limited company. Two years later George himself died, just months after the Lawnswood crematorium was opened. Fittingly his body was taken to Lawnswood where he became the tenth person to make use of the gas-fired incinerator.

There were no doubt many ladies present who shed a tear. In those early years Brays employed mainly women to carry out the intricate operations required. Most joined from school at the age of fourteen and left in their early twenties when they married; those who left with seven years service received a set of copper pans.

The pans would not however have been used to cook over any of Bray's burners. Until the early 1920s the jets were primarily used for lighting and the product range was supplemented by incandescent lighting burners. About

that time town gas was 'cleaned' and more use was made of jets for heating purposes in fires and central heating systems, whilst electricity took over the lighting load except in mines and other situations where acetylene was still used.

Ladies would be particularly noted for their achievements at Brays. The first qualified scientist to be employed by the company was Miss LM Sutton who qualified as a Chartered Engineer in 1920 and was later to become the firm's Chief Chemist. Miss Sutton would go on to be awarded the MBE for her contribution to the British war effort between 1939 and 1945. During the second world war Bray's made bomb fuses and gun sights.

After the war business was fairly steady until the 1950s when the introduction of better designed appliances and much cheaper gas led to a major increase in demand. George Bray, the youngest son of the founder died in 1952 and Clifford Bray the founder's eldest grandson took control. Sales increased from about £200,000 a year in 1955 to £500,000 in 1963 and to £700,000 in 1966. All that time Bray held about 95 per cent of the UK market and enjoyed substantial exports.

*Top left: Examples of natural gas modules. **Top right:** An exhibition from the 1950s. **Above right:** A gaslight from the early 1900s. **Left:** Bray Burners premises in the 1970s.*

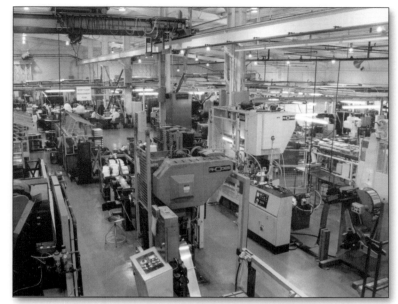

In 1958 Clifford Bray resigned as MD due to ill health and the founder's youngest grandsons George 'Geordie' and James 'Jim' Bray took the helm through the 1960s and 70s.

In 1962 natural gas had become available in Europe, firstly in Holland, Germany and France, leading to a requirement for aerated jets to replace non-aerated ones as a part of the conversion programme.

The conversion to natural gas in the UK began in 1967 and Bray's was technically well placed to meet the standards required. The company could not however hope to meet the full demand and the door was left open to competitors, particularly in the field of aerated burners of sheet metal construction. Nevertheless conversion had a dramatic effect on output. Between 1967 and 1969 sales increased

from £0.9 million to £2.6 million, of which more than half came from conversion products.

Whilst the company was fully committed to the UK Dutch and Italian competitors were beginning to make inroads in the European market.

There was a substantial trading loss in 1974 for the first and only time as high inflation damaged the business at a time when new premises had been acquired in both the UK and Germany. Profitability was restored however in 1975 and continued at a modest level following the end of the UK's conversion to natural gas in 1976.

Jim Bray retired in 1977 whilst his brother Geordie, though remaining as non-executive chairman, effectively retired two years later and the first outsider was appointed as Chief Executive. Shares in the company had begun to change hands as early as 1960, at first to the extended family and then to non-family directors. In 1969 the first large batch of shares, 55,000, was sold outside the family.

Five institutional shareholders acquired 40 per cent of ordinary share capital in 1981 and the company became a PLC 1983. Two years later Geordie Bray died, some four years after his brother Jim.

During the next decade the firm would diversify into tube-bending, oil burners and electric heating before refocusing on its core burner business in the 1990s. The company was sold to Findest SRL in 2000.

Today Bray's celebrated burners feature in millions of gas cookers, fires, boilers and pool heaters in the UK, Europe and the USA, installed in appliances made by household names such as Electrolux, Stoves, Baxi and Creda - and all thanks to that 21 year old entrepreneur, George Bray.

*Top left: The factory floor in the 1990s.*
*Left: An exhibition from the 1970s. **Below** A recent view of Bray Burners factory.*

# A moving tale

For those who enjoy the mystery, of the English language 'Pantechnicon' is a particularly attractive word. It's a word derived from classical Greek and literally means 'many arts' though in those far off days that word, or more accurately 'pantekhnikon', was then the name of a bazaar or market. In Victorian England the original Pantechnicon was a department store in London, a building in which it was intended to sell all kinds of artistic work, but which was eventually turned into a furniture store. That usage led in turn to the 'pantechnicon-van', a horse-drawn vehicle used to deliver furniture. Today pantechnicon is the name applied to large removal vans. And a removal firm which has a whole fleet of pantechnicons is McCarthy's Removals of Leeds.

Over a period of more than 30 years the blue-liveried lorries bearing the McCarthy name have become an increasingly familiar sight, not only around Leeds, but across the length and breadth of Britain.

*Top left: Company founder, Mick McCarthy.*
*Above right: The firm's first two vehicles.*
*Right: No 4 Lomond Place (the door with the demolition notice on it) was the firm's first headquarters. The vans were parked on the rubble outside. Below: Mick McCarthy with one of his first vehicles.*

Many readers may have also spotted an even older McCarthy pantechnicon. The firm's staff have repaired and rebuilt a 1937 Bedford furniture pantechnicon which is in regular use for promotional work and frequently displayed at vintage vehicle rallies across Yorkshire.

That fine vehicle was already almost 30 years old when the business was founded in 1968 by Michael 'Mick' McCarthy. Mick had earlier enjoyed a varied career as a window cleaner, lorry driver, painter, cleaner and mechanic before he started his own business doing general deliveries and removals.

For the first six months the new business was run from a terraced house in Lomond Place before moving to a listed building, Newton House, in Spencer Place from where the firm operated for the next seven years. Newton House was incidentally the very last long distance lorry drivers' hotel

Nor would bad weather delay deliveries. When arriving at a new house in Shropshire with a load of furniture the driver found the house surrounded by water after days of heavy rain. Many firms might have turned back in the face of a flood and tried again another day; but not McCarthy's. Like the famed Pony Express McCarthy's gets through whatever the obstacles in the way using skill and initiative. Despite the flood the furniture was delivered exactly as required by the client, though not without some pretty fancy work on behalf of the removal company. In the end McCarthy's had to unload the pantechnicon and use a local boat to ferry the household effects to the new house!

in Leeds. Since the early 1980s however McCarthy's has occupied, what was then a new, purpose built warehouse - the Depository in Meanwood Road. In later years, with ever increasing business another warehouse would come into use too.

But the removals business is not all about moving furniture: more exotic loads are frequently carried. McCarthy's motto might well have been 'we'll move anything anywhere'. Today that includes not just the kitchen sink but even the family car for those who don't want to make a journey to distant parts along unfamiliar roads: everything can go in the back of a van - even livestock, though not many clients want to move a dolphin. But McCarthy's have moved even those ever-smiling maritime mammals. It was McCarthy's that used to transport the dolphins to Flamingo Park laid on a hammock, carefully tended and kept moist in a McCarthy's van.

Inevitably, with hard work and a willingness to do anything, came growth. Before too long Mick had a small fleet of vans - and they would work at any hour of the day or night if required. In those still-early years McCarthy's once had no fewer than 12 vans working on a Saturday night moving scenery across the country for a theatre company for the next week's show; it was of course vital that the firm delivered on time so that the show could go on, and they never failed to deliver.

**Top:** *McCarthys removal vans in the early 1970s.*
**Right:** *The firm's second premises in Spencer Place, Leeds.*

Meanwhile, over the decades since the firm was founded, many things have changed. Tea chests which were once universally used in the industry for packing household goods have all but disappeared, alongside the newspaper once used for wrapping and sack cloth used to protect furniture. Today by contrast cardboard cartons have replaced tea chests, plastic bubble wrap is used for 'fragiles' whilst purpose-made covers are used to protect furniture. The McCarthy packing service ensures that every fragile possession is individually wrapped and protected; silverware is wrapped in acid free tissue, clothes and linen are packed into purpose-built wardrobes which keep clothes clean and crease free during the move, whilst

china and glasses are wrapped in white paper before being placed in purpose-made cartons; mattress sleeves are used to ensure complete protection for them during the move and all bedding is packed into linen bags whilst specialist items, such as clocks and antiques, are given particular attention.

Yet another change has been the opportunity to have household effects packed into sealed containers which can then be placed in secure storage for later delivery to a new address.

Such professionalism is all a long way from the 'Dad, do you know the piano's on my foot?' image of the famous PG Tips advert featuring the Mr Shifter and his hapless son, the pair of chimps who turn to be a pair of chumps. Moving house these days is not a job for well meaning amateurs.

And its not just domestic 'flitting' that McCarthy's undertake. Today the business also includes general transport of furniture from manufacturers to retail outlets, and subsequent deliveries from the shop to the customer.

Office removals and document storage using the world's leading software for document and archive storage are also a large part of the McCarthy operation, as well as offering high security storage to museums and others for fine art and antiquities. Nor is the UK the limit of McCarthy's reach, with shipping regularly arranged to such countries as the USA, Canada and Australia.

Over the years clients have included TV personalities and sports stars, a service provided with such discretion and confidentiality that even after very many years Mick McCarthy still won't give away any of the domestic secrets which he has learned about the rich and the famous.

One story that Mick is willing to reveal however occurred in the early 1970s when he moved a client from Leeds to Essex. Dolphins were no problem at all but Mick

*Top right: A van loaded for theatre work in the early 1970s. Notice the props sticking out of the front. **Above right:** In 2002 the firm moved the contents of Brampton House. The contents had not been moved since 1920 and the whole move took a week. The old Bedford van is the oldest working vehicle in England.*
***Left:*** *Moving an exhibition around the country.*

got quite a shock on discovering that his client kept a full grown lion as a pet in the back garden.

But not everyone it seems actually wants to move home. Mick once moved a customer 250 miles from Leeds to Brighton - but when she got there she changed her mind and McCarthy's brought her back to Leeds the following day.

The customer is of course always right, and always bearing that in mind has been one of the reasons that McCarthy's has continued to grow. The firm aims to provide customers with a removal and storage service of such high quality and value for money that they can recommend McCarthy's to their friends, families and colleagues with total confidence.

From just two or three staff at the outset this once small business now has around 40 members of staff, all of whom have undergone intensive training at McCarthy's own 'in-house' training school and many of whom have been accredited by the Movers Institute.

Mick's wife and his eldest son, a second Michael McCarthy, are both involved; Mrs McCarthy acting as company secretary and doing the accounts whilst son Michael now takes care of marketing and operations.

And what of the future? Though removals will no

doubt remain backbone of the McCarthy enterprise the demand for high security storage is continually rising: in response the firm intends to develop that part of the business and provide far more of those special facilities in the coming years.

Though many things have changed down the years, the size of the vans, packaging materials and the use of computers, not to mention prices which have risen from just 17/6 per hour (75p) in 1968 to £40 -per hour in 2002, some things never change. One one of the most important things which has not changed is McCarthy's permanent commitment to quality - a commitment which has been impressing satisfied clients ever since that day when Mick McCarthy started his small business which was destined to achieve such great things.

*Top right and above left: Carefully packing the contents of a house for removal. Above right: Inside the storage warehouse. Left: The Depository on Meanwood Road, Leeds, home to the firm since the early 1980s.*

# *Lowe name - high standards*

owe Engineering - George E Lowe Ltd to give the
company its official title - will be a familiar name
to those who regularly pass along Kirkstall Road.
The Lowe family started trading in Leeds during
the early 1930s and since then their engineering company
has pioneered integrated technical solutions for its
multitude of clients across a broad range of critical
industrial applications.

The company's early focus was on serving the petrol distribution industry to whom it began by supplying storage
tanks, pipelines and reconditioned pumps. The 1930s were
not the best of times to embark upon a new business.
The hungry thirties as they were known was a time of
terrible poverty arising from the world trade depression
which had begun in 1929. Despite that dreadful depression however some sectors of the economy still
continued to move forward, not least the petroleum
industry, as the internal combustion engine continued
to supersede horses and steam power- even if that
growth was somewhat slower than it would otherwise
have been.

For individuals the start of the second world war in
1939 presaged tragedy, for industry however it was the
kick start which the world economy needed. Unemployment ended almost overnight, and the demands of a
war economy
stimulated both
production and
innovation to heights
never before achieved.

Driven by the demands
of the 1940s war effort
Lowe Engineering
perfected specialist
welding and machining
skills in aluminium
and steel; after the war
that capability enabled
the company to further
develop and market its
own range of products.
During the early 1960s

*Above right: A steam
and water sampling
system. Right: The
firm's old Burley Wood
Works.*

Peter Lowe, who by the start of the new millennium would
have become company chairman, had the vision to collab-
orate with the Central Electricity Generating Board's
Scientific Services Division to jointly develop a range of
probes, high quality heat exchangers, coolers and
specialised sampling equipment for power station boilers.

Integrating that range of equipment into Steam and Water
Analysis System Solutions enabled the company to develop
an export trade on a global basis, successfully tendering
for major new power station projects in India, Hong Kong,
China and Africa.

standards of workmanship, meeting codes required by Lloyds, the MOD and ASME. Skilled welders using approved weld procedures construct, amongst other things, pressure and storage vessels for liquids such as nitro-glycerine and nitric acid as well as recompression chambers for divers and other fabrications for marine applications.

In 1987 the company was one of the first in its field to obtain registration under the prestigious ISO9001 standard covering design, manufacture and installation.

The company has become adept at providing designs for, and working with, overseas contractors and end users - many having their own specialised requirements or technical standards, applications, difficulties and not least local support for technical and after-sales service. Lowe now has systems working in power plants as far afield as South Africa, India, the Caribbean, the Middle East, SE Asia, Hong Kong and China.

Today the company's management team offers fully integrated solutions to its clients; no matter what the enormity of the task, it is viewed simply as a new challenge by this responsive company which prides itself on consistently achieving remarkable things incredibly quickly, and to consistently high standards.

*Above left: Recompression chambers.*
*Below: The firm's new building.*

International recognition as a leading design authority for a wide range of boiler - water and steam, process liquids and gasses, in applications ranging from power generation to chemical processing plants - spurred dramatic rates of business growth during the 1980s. Additional manufacturing capacity in the form of a new purpose built facility in Kirkstall Road was completed in three stages to cope with that increase in demand.

Constantly seeking new challenges the company would further develop its expertise and begin to move into environmental monitoring, data capture and reporting systems. By the early 21st century it was able to offer leading edge computer solutions that complimented its analysis systems. These would consist of a range of process instruments, 'annunciators' and recorders, installed in fully lit, heated and ventilated control cabins.

The second area in which the company has developed particular expertise is in high quality fabrications in aluminium, stainless steels and exotic alloys. These are supplied to industrial, marine and petrochemical markets for use in applications which require high

# *Building a reputation*

Horsforth folk are used to seeing scarlet-liveried lorries with the slogan 'Building Supplies' above the driver's cab with the company name 'J & L Marshall' in larger lettering. The business was founded when a couple of jobbing joiners, Jack Marshall and his uncle, Leonard Marshall, decided to take a gamble. 'We'd got a bit fed up working for other people' Jack recalls. Leonard, Jack's guide and mentor, died several years ago.

It was in 1958 that the duo began their business from a small workshop on Long Row, Horsforth. Work began slowly before their reputation for reliable and highly skilled work began to bring them more and more business. The Marshalls moved on to premises in Troy Hill, Horsforth with more room and better facilities in 1970; though they were still primarily joiners for some years they were

*Below: Where it all began, the Marshall's first premises in Long Row, Horsforth.*

undertakers too. Jack still has his old top hat from those days and his memories, 'It was a sad business basically' he says 'But you have to be able to have a laugh now and then, and undertakers have a sense of humour like everybody else'.

But undertaking wasn't a way of life, or death, that Jack enjoyed and he gave it up and in 1975 took another gamble buying a site in New Road Side, Horsforth, on the main Leeds to Horsforth Road. There was a large wooden workshop and several lock-up garages on the site when Jack signed 'the biggest cheque in my life ... I nearly had a heart attack - but that came later'.

The old wooden structure came down, offices were built, more land was developed for storage, a larger workshop was built, a builders merchant depot constructed and shop premises fronting the main road were bought and turned into a hardware shop. The firm took on skilled workers and added a small general building section, with joiners, bricklayers and apprentices.

been responsible for some outstanding examples of the bricklayers art.

Dave Goodban's nickname was given to him to distinguish him from 'Young Dave', Jack's son, David Marshall, who joined the company in 1972 and has since taken on the business; Jack, now in his 70s, is however still putting in full days.

Other members of the original team were Jack's wife Betty and Leonard's wife Nell who did all of the office work. David's wife Karen later took over the running of the office and was joined by Carol Geyer.

Now Jack gradually found himself spending more time acting as an intermediary between local tradesmen and the big suppliers of bulk building materials. This was how the company found its niche in the local building industry.

In the 1990s J&L Marshall extended its business in the area by taking over and developing premises in Ellar Ghyll, Bradford Road, Otley, from where it also provides building materials to the trade and to DIY enthusiasts. That part of the Marshalls 'empire' is run by Robin Shuttleworth who joined the firm in 1996 and who would subsequently become a partner in the business.

At the beginning of the 21st century Marshalls had become one of the areas best known suppliers of building materials. Some 70 per cent of the firm's business comes from builders the other 30 per cent to DIYers - who would often end up asking Jack to put right what they started in the first place!

The longest serving employee is David Goodban, who joined the firm from school in 1965. 'Big Dave' is a highly skilled joiner but also able to turn is hand to just about any job in the building trade. Tony Rawnsley, chief bricklayer, joined Marshall's in 1984, and has

The firm now employs some 20 people. Chris Perkis runs the Horsforth depot, Bryan Whitham the hardware shop and Paul Fairburn, who joined the firm in 1988, is a particularly valued member of the building team.

With a quiet smile Jack Marshall looks back with a mixture of pride and surprise, 'Aye, we haven't done so bad' he says, 'We'll just have to keep going on, under David and Robin, just doing our best, that's all we have ever done, and all we ever wanted to do.'

*Top left:* The company's current premises when bought by Jack Marshall in 1975. ***Above left:*** Marshall's Hardware shop. ***Below:*** Part of the J & L Marshall fleet.

# Wm Dodgson & Son - A final service

**A**ccording to the old adage there are only two certainties in life - death and taxes. The very rich and the very poor may avoid taxes, but none of us avoid death. And if the manner of our passing may matter little to us once we are gone, it is very important to the bereaved.

The bereaved face a task made doubly difficult by their grief. During the course of the 19th century the demand for sympathetic, skilled and knowledgeable help led inexorably to the growth of the profession of undertaker, a profession which in its early days almost invariable drew its recruits from the ranks of joiners who, in addition to their other work, also made coffins.

*Above: Mr Lindley Dodgson. **Right:** This photograph was taken after William Dodgson, the senior partner in the firm had been installed as National President of the NAFD in 1968. He is pictured in the centre, with his son Martin on his right and his father William on his left. **Below:** The first Rolls-Royce hearses and limousines, from the 1930s.*

One of the most respected funeral directors in Yorkshire, and one with a history going back to the early years of Queen Victoria's reign, is that of Leeds-based Wm Dodgson & Son.

The firm of Wm Dodgson & Son was founded in 1842 by a joiner and undertaker, William Dodgson, who worked from a joiners shop in Shannon Street. He was succeeded by John Dodgson who, in addition to joinery and undertaking, also built rows of back to back houses in

partnership with local builders. The streets in which the houses were built were named after his relatives: indeed Ada Crescent and Bertha Street were named after his daughters. Before long the success of his business led to the need for new premises and the firm moved to Beckett Street.

After John's death in 1938 his sons, William and Lindley, succeeded him. They moved the business again, to Cowper Grove, into purpose built premises which included a chapel of rest. The chapel of rest was a pioneering concept in Leeds at the time, before then the deceased usually remained at home until the time of the funeral.

The two brothers were then joined by William's son, who was also called William, and bought their first motorised fleet including a Rolls-Royce hearse. This was possible due to the continued success of the company achieved through the quality of its personal service and traditional values and courtesy. At the same time the joinery side of the business was adapted to specialise in the construction of coffins. Lindley Dodgson died in 1953 but three years later the fifth generation of Dodgsons joined the company. Martin Dodgson was 16 when he first began working for the firm and was the first member of the family to be sent on a two and a half year course in London to study every aspect of funeral directing.

The business expanded and soon outgrew the Cowper Grove premises and moved to its present site in Lupton Avenue, Harehills where today it still serves the Leeds area. The property has a number of chapels of rest and catering facilities.

William Dodgson lived long enough to see these developments, but sadly died in 1971. During his life he had served as National President of the National Association of Funeral Directors, a position taken up by his son some years later. The business continued to prosper under the expert guidance of his son William, and grandson Martin. Martin Dodgson served a term as National President of the British Institute of Embalmers; from 1968 he also served as a member of Leeds City Council and was accorded the honour of being Lord Mayor of Leeds in 1983. He was one of the youngest Lord Mayors that Leeds has ever had. Martin ended his active association with the company in 1985; thereafter the traditions and standards so long established and without parallel in the city of Leeds have continued and are maintained today by the current qualified and committed staff. Although the company is no longer run by the Dodgson family, Martin retains an active interest in its progress into the new millennium.

Today the name of Wm Dodgson & Son, Funeral Directors and Monumental Masons, is even better known than in the past: in its more recent years the company has acquired additional premises at Selby Road, Halton, Harrogate Road, Moortown as well as in High Street, Kippax and at Middleton Park Circus, Middleton. At all of the premises the standard of

service remains the highest that generations of experience can offer.

***Top left:*** *A company invoice dated 1919.* ***Left:*** *Mr Martin Dodgson, one of the youngest Lord Mayors of Leeds, wearing his mayoral chain of office.* ***Below:*** *The Wm Dodgson and Son's fleet of hearses and limousines.*

# Stocks and shares

These days an awful lot of us own stocks and shares. And folk in Leeds may well have acquired theirs through the long-established stockbroking firm of Redmayne-Bentley.

It was Christmas 1875 when John Redmayne embarked upon the great adventure of setting up as a stockbroker on his own account at the Leeds Stock Exchange. From that small beginning today's Redmayne-Bentley has become one of the UK's leading independent private client stockbrokers.

It was the Great Railways Boom which brought the Stock Exchange to Leeds in the mid 19th century and which was the foundation of its success. John Redmayne's early triumphs were bound up with dealing in railway shares for private investors. His reputation grew and it was as an 'expert on rails' that, on a visit to the USA, he was introduced to a group of New York brokers.

Although interest in railways eventually declined John Redmayne thrived because of his overriding

*Below: Famous stock-market adversaries, the Bull and the Bear come together to launch Redmayne-Bentley's Stocks and Shares shop in Albion Street, Leeds. **Right:** An example of a stock market trading floor.*

passion was to provide a first class highly efficient and above all friendly service to his clients: that philosophy would prove to be winner.

The firm went on growing, and able new partners ensured the firm's reputation flourished. A major landmark was passed in 1965 when Gavin Loudon, father of the present senior partner, Keith Loudon, organised the merger of Redmayne & Co with FW Bentley & Co.

By the time of the 'Big Bang' for the London Stock Exchange in 1986, which introduced far reaching changes to stockbroking in the UK, the firm had to make some difficult choices. Conventional wisdom dictated that regional firms should join up with others to become large conglomerates,

through the Internet - but always with the addition of help and advice for clients who prefer a more personal touch. The firm was also a prime mover in initiating a London Stock Exchange educational campaign to demystify share investment and tell the public about the long-term benefits of owning shares.

Another important development came in 2001 with the opening of the Redmayne Stocks and Shares Shop in Albion Street: a first for the firm and a first for Leeds. There shoppers can have a chat, drink a cup of coffee and buy or sell shares - an echo of Jonathan's Coffee House where the London Stock Market began.

Since 1995, when the Investors Chronicle magazine began an annual awards scheme, Redmayne-Bentley would be a consistent award winner: 'Best Regional Broker', 'Best Portfolio manger' and 'Best Innovating Broker' - and not least the coveted top award of 'UK Stockbroker of the Year'.

Today's partners hold true to the course set by John Redmayne so many years ago. And nothing could express that course better than the firm's proud declaration on its logo: 'Your Friend on the Stock Exchange'.

focusing on either the 'top end' of the market, advising wealthy clients, or offer a bargain basement, no frills service to smaller clients. The partners of Redmayne-Bentley and its clients felt differently. The three partners decided they could stay independent by continuing to offer a full range of services to the firms loyal and growing list of private clients. They were proved right.

Though Redmayne-Bentley's commission charges were not always the lowest they were and would remain competitive: but above all it was the firm's strong Yorkshire roots, its efficient and friendly service and its expert advice that enabled the firm not just to survive but to prosper and attract increasing numbers of clients.

The firm's reputation began to spread across the UK and, as it did, teams of stockbrokers in other parts of the country, attracted by the Redmayne style of doing business made approaches asking if they might join up. And so the branch network was born.

Since then Redmayne-Bentley has grown into the UK's leading independent stockbroker with 30 branches throughout the UK from Scotland to the South coast.

Although traditions remain strong the firm has never been afraid of change and has often been a leader and innovator. Many years ago it was the first firm in Leeds to install a teleprinter. The firm was also one of the first to try out television advertising.

The same is true today: Redmayne-Bentley were amongst the first stockbrokers to introduce on-line share dealing

**Top left:** *Senior Partner, Keith Loudon, receives a UK Equity Award for Best Discretionary Broker.*
**Above left:** *Keith Loudon and TV gardening celebrity Charlie Dimmock launch the London Stock Exchange's Share Aware Campaign to help people understand the benefits of investing in shares.* **Below:** *Celebrating success! Over the years Redmayne-Bentley have won awards like this one from Investors' Chronicle, covering the entire range of their service.*

# *Wood you believe it?*

**W**ho says that craftsmanship is dead? Today, businesses that are seeking custom-made, architect-designed top quality office fittings and furniture know exactly where to look: they head for the Larchfield Works in Larchfield Road and the premises of the internationally renowned firm of specialist joiners, W Button & Co Ltd.

Walter Button was born in Hunslet, Leeds in 1928. At the age of 14 he became an apprentice joiner working in the maintenance department at John Fowler's in Hunslet; he volunteered for service in the RAF at the age of 17 in which he spent the next three years. In 1948 whilst completing his training after being demobbed he met his future wife Joyce; she was then a private secretary working for a wholesale chemist. The pair married in 1950 and had their first son, Steven, the following year and their second son, Richard, in 1955.

**Above:** *The company premises in Larchfirld Road in the late 1960s.* **Right:** *Office staff circa 1980s.* **Below:** *An interior view of the factory.*

Deciding that self employment promised a better future than working for someone else Walter's business began in 1952 from lock up shop premises in Seacroft which he rented from the Leeds City Corporation. Walter used his experience as a master joiner to give quotations and do the materials buying as well as producing quality joinery; meanwhile Joyce used her experience as a secretary to look after invoicing, the accounts and telephone enquiries. Unlike today, in the computer age, when photocopiers and computer design and fax machines are indispensable, in those early days drawings and instructions were given in longhand on foolscap paper.

At first the business was mostly basic joinery. Walter started out by fitting private houses with fitted furniture, he

moved on to making display stands and progressed to manufacturing wooden cabinets for one armed bandits.

By 1958 the small firm had four members of staff: Joyce Button doing the office work and accounts and three joiners, including Walter. That year they moved to Waddingtons Yard Crown Point and in the mid 1960s moved once more, to Stafford Street in Hunslet, before having a purpose built factory erected in Larchfield Road, Hunslet in 1968. By dint of hard work, and even harder selling, backed by impeccable standards the company had succeeded in becoming the largest manufacturer of snooker tables, as seen on TV, in the country and had moved on to making school and laboratory furniture and finally into the manufacture of specialist doors, including bullet proof doors, fire doors and acoustically rated doors in addition to bespoke office furniture.

The new Larchfield Works was located on an acre of land with 26,000 sq ft of factory and office space. Everything was going well until the mid 1970s. In 1977 a disastrous fire destroyed half the factory along with 1,500 snooker tables and the laboratory furniture for a whole new hospital in Dubai. Frighteningly this happened on the first week of a firemen's strike; fortunately the fire was attended by police and army fire-fighters and their Green Goddesses who together managed to save half the factory.

Fortunately the business was strong enough to rise from the ashes, helped by the unstinting efforts of its workforce. Today production includes doors and doorsets for use in banks, offices, hotels and boardrooms as well as one-off office furniture and reception desks. The firm also specialised in various types of wall panelling used in

boardrooms, conference centres and moveable wall systems, specialist mouldings, architraves and skirting. All the joinery made by the firm is produced to order working from architects' drawings or detailed instructions from commissioning companies.

At the start of the 21st century the firm employs 34 staff - four directors, three office staff plus its joiners and machine men. Many of those staff and tradesmen have worked for the firm for more than 20 years.

Both Steven and Richard Button would work for the company before starting their own DIY shop in 1985. Both remain directors of the firm, though while Steven's career remains within another industry Richard, a joiner by trade, and who also attended college to additionally study electronics and plumbing rejoined the company as its Works Director in 1999.

After more than half a century in the joinery business W Button Ltd is a firm whose past and present prove conclusively that, in Yorkshire at least, craftsmanship is far from being dead!

*Top right:* Finishing a boardroom table.
*Left:* A birds eye view of W Button & Co.Ltd.
*Below:* Walter Button discussing a progress report with Tracy Sanderson.

# *Saying it with flowers*

Undoubtedly the best known florists in Leeds is Brethericks in Harrogate Road.

The firm was founded in 1946 when Ronald Bretherick and his wife Kathleen began trading as RW & K Bretherick. Ronald had recently been discharged from the forces whilst Kathleen already had a career as a florist.

During the war years Kathleen had a job buying fruit and vegetables for six shops in West Yorkshire - all of which were run by women. In the 1930s when Kathleen left school there were few jobs about but she managed to get an apprenticeship in a plant nursery before deciding to take up floristry. In those days there were no Colleges offering floristry courses so she had to gain experience where she could.

*Top left:* Founders Kathleen and Ronald Bretherick.
*Right:* Ronald Bretherick outside their first shop.
*Below:* A display for the 1953 Leeds Flower Show.

The spur to start out on their own came when the shops Kathleen had been working for were put up for sale and she and Ron bought two of them, they also bought a small second hand van which cost them £300 and which let in water when it rained - and whose rear door was secured with a length of string. The shop in Harehills Road, was sold four years later however allowing the couple to concentrate their efforts.

Kathleen was a floral designer whilst Ron did all the buying, getting in the flowers, fruit and veg from the wholesale markets.

From 1946 until 1957 the couple's shop would be located at 94A Harrogate Road; they then moved to 116, staying there until 1983, the year in which a branch at Moortown was opened, and when the main shop moved to its present location at 178/180 Harrogate Road. It was hard work but the couple were ambitious and willing to work even

on Sundays - something which resulted in increased business when the firm became popular with Leeds' Jewish population which regularly held its weddings on Sundays

Always wanting to do better Kathleen heard of the Society of Floristry in the mid 1950s and from then on studied relentlessly, gaining a Diploma from the Society in 1957; she little realised that one day she would become President of the Society.

Kathleen would teach floristry part-time at Wakefield Technical College for 25 years; daughter Sandra Moss, not to be outdone, has taught at Leeds College of Art and Design for even longer.

Expert in all manner of flower arrangements Brethericks cater for everyone and every occasion: from corporate clients to individuals just passing by, and from happy occasions such as weddings to sad ones like funerals.

Sadly Ron Bretherick had died in 1968 leaving Kathleen to continue on her own helped by her staff, and her daughter Sandra, who had joined the business in the early 1960s.

Despite that sadness life as a florist did have its lighter moments: on one occasion a burglar broke into the shop and kindly left his GCSE timetable with his name on it next to the till! Once the firm's clients who had

ordered red and white flowers changed their minds after the flower displays had been set out and demanded blue instead: nothing daunted Kathleen and her staff grabbed some flower paint spray and, like a scene from Alice in Wonderland, painted the offending blooms blue. On another occasion a lady rang to complain about the amount of soil in her sink: she had been told to water the plant from the bottom and had turned the pot upside down in the sink and tried to put water through the hole in the base of the pot!

Fortunately most customers understand rather more about plant care. Today Sandra Moss runs the business though Kath is still involved, albeit from semi-retirement, and writes books for student florists whilst Sandra offers flower arranging classes and demonstrations encouraging the general public to appreciate flowers and how to care for plants.

The firm changed its name to the simpler 'Brethericks' in the 1980s.

Today's staff of 12 have between them 118 years of experience with the business, whilst others have trained with Brethericks and moved on to open their own florists' businesses.

Despite competition from supermarkets business is still blooming thanks to Brethericks' top quality customer service and products - flowers and flower arrangements which ensure that the firm's clients always come back again.

*Top left: RW & K Bretherick's shop and flat pictured in 1970.*
*Top right: Mrs Sandra Moss and Mrs Kathleen Bretherick.*
*Left: The firms Harrogate Road shop today.*

# A *treat in store*

Over the last fifty years we've all become used to seeing a very high standard of quality shop fittings. One local firm which has risen to national prominence in that specialist field is Lynn & Jones Ltd with its headquarters at Falcon House in Holbeck.

Lynn & Jones was founded in 1948 as a partnership between Robert Lynn and Ivor Jones.

Ivor served his National Service in the Black Watch REME, during which time he was posted to Greece and whilst there he supervised German prisoners of war and constructed a complete orphans home. On returning home Ivor rejoined S&H Collins in North Street, Leeds. It was there where he had served his apprenticeship, and where Robert 'Bob' Lynn was the workshop foreman. Within a few weeks Ivor had decided to start his own business and a few months later Bob joined him.

At first Lynn & Jones took on any work which had to do with wood and for which clients would pay promptly.

A small lock up shop was rented in Burley, but within six months space was becoming a problem and a move to larger premises became necessary. A long association with Walter Street, Kirkstall Road now began in the shadow of the railway viaduct.

Norman Liversedge arrived as the firm's first employee; later, after many years of loyal service, he would

go on to form his own shop fitting company. Within eight years the number of employees had increased to ten.

The most notable of the new employees would be Douglas Harrison who joined the firm straight from school and became its first apprentice. (Other than a short break for National Service Doug Harrison would work for Lynn & Jones all his working life becoming Works Director in 1984, a position he would enjoy for two decades).

Clientele soon increased following recommendations, especially amongst local traders such as HG Grahams, Stylo Shoes and Fyffes and fitted furniture.

A chance meeting in a local timber yard with the head architect for Timothy White and Taylors Chemists, led to the fitting out of complete new shops. In the mid 1960s when Timothy White's was swallowed up by the much larger Boots the Chemists a new relationship was forged with that large multi-chain national chemists, a relationship

*Top left:* Mr Ivor Jones as an apprentice. ***Above:*** *Mr Ivor Jones serving in Greece.* ***Left:*** *The directors celebrating the retirement of Mrs Mary McLean, accounts manager, in 1989. Clockwise from the top left - Mr Christopher Jones, Mr David Lynn, Mr Ivor Jones, Mrs Mary McLean and Mr Trevor Jones.*

specialist market. Over the next 20 years the company went on to fit out many leisure venues for such companies as Rank, First Leisure and Mecca.

Expansion became possible in 1976 with the purchase of 15 Walter Street, followed later by 19 Walter Street (formerly the Charles Tinkness Concrete works).

Ivor Jones' younger son Christopher joined the firm in 1977, whilst a new name, Darren Brook, joined the company in the 1980s eventually becoming a director of the firm.

Robert Lynn retired in 1984, followed by Ivor Jones in 1992. David Lynn left the business in 1997 to pursue other interests in Cornwall. The third generation of the Jones family joined the family firm in 2000.

April 2001 saw the company move to Kenneth Street, Holbeck overlooking the main artery to Leeds the M621 where a very large investment has been made in hi-tech machines.

Today Lynn & Jones' 80 odd employees would certainly agree that they've come a long way from that tiny lock up shop in Burley Place.

which would still be flourishing in the 21st century.

Meanwhile, whilst the relationship with Timothy White's was still developing, another large client Great Universal Stores began commissioning work from Lynn & Jones.

The extra activity meant that once again more work space was needed. The purchase of the Viaduct Coach Building Works in Walter Street followed in 1956. At the same time many new woodworking machines were bought from, a local retailer who had decided to close its shopfitting department and dispose of its machines.

In 1965 Bob Lynn's only son, David, finished his education and joined the firm to serve a full apprenticeship. The following year Ivor Jones' eldest son, Trevor, finished his schooldays and moved on to the Leeds College of Building which he attended full time before himself joining the company in the Drawing Office.

The early 1970s saw the opening of many new night clubs and discotheques which in turn saw Lynn & Jones develop this

*Top left:* Wm Morrison. *Left:* Lynn & Jones works, prior to demolition, ERE Building. *Below:* A Lynn & Jones vehicle.

# Brooke North -
# A modern law firm with an historic past.

After 70 years as a solicitor John Thackrah died, aged 93, in 1903. Shortly after that the firm moved to North British & Mercantile Buildings in East Parade.

Joshua B Brooke was killed in March 1914 in a hunting accident when following the Bramham Moor Hunt.
A memorial to him appears in St John's Church Moor Allerton.

On JB Brooke's death Herbert Dyer, who had joined the practice a short time before, acquired the practice. At the time Herbert Dyer was earning just £200 per year as an assistant solicitor with the firm and had insufficient capital to buy the firm outright; fortunately he was able to come to terms with the widow to pay for the practice over a period of ten years, though in fact he was able to pay for it in six years, just before Mrs Brooke's death in 1919.

During the first world war Wilfred Goodwin joined the firm as an office boy; he would go on to eventually become senior partner, acquiring the firm on the death of Herbert Dyer when the firm changed its name to Brooke, Dyer and Goodwin. Wilfred Goodwin would recall that in the days when he started the firm had just six, all male, employees, including a 78 year old clerk named Sam Waddington who seemed to have no job other than to chew tobacco and write out or 'engross' deeds by hand onto sheepskins.

The firm of Brooke, Dyer and Goodwin merged with North and Sons in 1970, the firm then becoming known as Brooke, North and Goodwin.

North & Sons had a history almost as long as 'Brookes'. The founder of that firm was William North who had

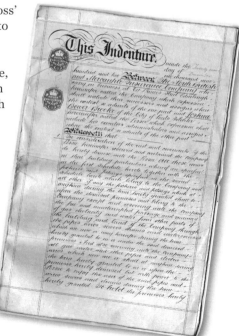

I n recent years Leeds has become one of the most important centres for legal work in the country. Brooke North is a modern commercial law practice, located in Crown House, Great George Street, but its roots go back to the middle of the 19th century.

It was in 1833 that John Thackrah started his own firm.

Joshua Bower Brooke joined the practice in 1874; his brother, JA Brooke, joined the practice some time later though died before his brother. In those years the firm occupied offices at number 1 East Parade.

*Above:* *Joshua Bower Brooke.*
*Right:* *A lease from 1902 between North British and Mercantile and JB Brooke.*

were William Hannam, Reader Whittell, Arthur Holmes and lastly Cecil Hannam who had recently joined his father in the practice.

In 1924 the firm moved its offices to City Chambers in Infirmary Street where it would remain until 1965.

Cecil Hannam would run the firm alone throughout the period of the second world war before being joined in turn by his sons Martin Hannam and Hugh Hannam.

In 1965 North & Sons moved from Infirmary Street to Yorkshire House in East Parade, premises which were also occupied by Brooke Dyer & Goodwin - a proximity which would soon lead to a merger.

The firm expanded considerably during the 1970s and 1980s and acquired an enviable reputation as one of the leading law firms in the City.

In 1995 Brooke North moved to its new purpose built offices at Crown House, Great George Street. The firm has continued to grow under its current management and now has 17 partners.

Brooke North specialises in providing a top class commercial legal service to businesses whether local, national or international, ably combining the best traditions of the past with up to the minute skills and expertise.

qualified as an attorney and solicitor at the age of 39 in 1849. William North went into practice on his own account in Leeds in 1854, at first in Park Row before moving to 4 East Parade where the firm continued to practice until 1924. William North died in 1883, his last will and testament being so complex that at least three applications had to be made to the courts to interpret it, the last occasion being as late as 1969 some 86 years after his death!

William North's firm had become North & Sons in the 1860s when two of his six sons, John and Arthur, had joined him. Arthur however soon left, leaving the firm to John North.
At the time of John North's death in 1915 the partners

*Top left: A company cheque dated 1931.*
*Left: Crown House , Great George Street, Leeds, today's premises of Brooke North, Solicitors .*
*Below: Members of the current management team at Brooke North.*

# A longstanding ovation

Puccini, Verdi and Mussorgsky may not be common names in Leeds, but happily for opera fans they have certainly become much more familiar than they once were.

For almost a quarter of a century, since 1978, Opera North has been the national opera company for the North - the largest opera company in England outside London. The Company has established itself as one of the leading arts organisations in the country, and as one of the most exciting and imaginative opera companies in Europe. Its innovative approach to programming and performance style has been widely acknowledged through a number of prestigious awards, including an international Emmy in 2000 for 'Gloriana: A Film', made for the BBC and based on Opera North's landmark production. The Company is also renowned as a strong advocate of lesser known works and as a champion of musical theatre.

From its home at the Grand Theatre, the Company has actively challenged established perceptions of opera. It has collaborated with other artists and companies, and created work in a range of media, including film and photography. The critically-acclaimed Chorus and versatile Orchestra also perform independently. Creativity and the development of individual skills are important throughout the Company, from the performers to the highly talented team of technical, production and management staff.

The Education department is a key part of the Company's work, using opera to inspire and develop creativity in young people, and the wider community.

The work of the opera company is made possible by direct support from both the Arts Council of England and local authorities - led by Leeds City Council, which also holds a free annual 'Opera in the Park' event with Opera North at Temple Newsam, attended by up to 40,000 people. Other funding comes from sponsorship from the private sector, the Friends of Opera North (who alone have raised almost half a million pounds) and the Opera North Foundation. By the millennium, more than three million people had already attended Opera North events, and by the Company's 25th birthday in 2003, a great many more will have joined them - a truly remarkable achievement.

**Above:** *Josephine Barstow in the role of Queen Elizabeth I in Opera North's 1996 production of 'Gloriana' by Benjamin Britten.* **Below:** *A performance of 'Elixir of Love' by Gaetano Donizetti, 2000.*

© Stephen Vaughan

© Stephen Vaughan

# Northern Ballet Theatre

Formed in 1969 and originally housed in the Zion Institute in Manchester, Northern Ballet Theatre was the first national ballet company in England to be based outside London. NBT now resides in the West Park Centre, Leeds and tours throughout the UK - from Cardiff to Edinburgh, London to Belfast and everywhere in between - for at least 28 weeks each year reaching an annual audience of over 175,000. The company has also established an international reputation having toured to China, Greece, Turkey and the Czech and Slovak Republic in recent years.

NBT is currently made up of 34 classically trained dancers from countries all over the world including: Brazil, Japan, South Africa, Australia, USA, Canada and the UK and Europe. NBT also comprises an orchestra of approximately 30 players and an administrative and technical support team of over 40. Alongside the UK's most extensive dance tour NBT education run a programme of creative activities in schools, colleges and community centres - committed to opening the world of dance to those traditionally excluded from it. In the past year over 9,000 people, of all ages and from all walks of life, participated in events, with nearly a third of these coming from the West Yorkshire region.

Over the years NBT has built an enviable reputation for accessible, strong narrative ballets, producing a variety of stimulating new works that challenge NBT's dancers and provide audiences with a wide-range of quality dance experience. Many of those responsible for the creation of these productions and in some cases the productions themselves have been acknowledged with awards from BAFTA, Laurence Olivier Awards, Dance and Dancers Magazine, Manchester Evening News Awards and the Royal Philharmonic Music Awards.

In August 2001 Canadian-born David Nixon was appointed Artistic Director and in his first season added two critically acclaimed productions to NBT's repertoire: a full-length narrative ballet, *Madame Butterfly* and a programme of dances set to Gershwin songs, *I Got Rhythm - the genius of Gershwin* ® *in song and dance*. His first complete new work for NBT, *Wuthering Heights*, a collaboration with composer Claude-Michel Schönberg, known throughout the musical-theatre world for his West End hits *Les Misérables, Martin Guerre* and *Miss Saigon* - had its World Première at the Alhambra Theatre in Bradford in September 2002.

Future new works include the UK première of *Beauty and the Beast,* Birgit Scherzer's *Requiem* and *A Midsummer Night's Dream*, a new full-length work by David Nixon. NBT productions are always premièred in Yorkshire.

Over the past few years Northern Ballet Theatre and Phoenix Dance Theatre have worked on plans to construct a new £9million headquarters on Quarry Hill in Leeds city centre. These plans are now in their final stages and on completion will result in the largest centre for dance in the United Kingdom outside London. Their Royal Highnesses, the Earl and Countess of Wessex made clear their support for NBT and Phoenix Dance Theatre when they attended the launch of the final fundraising campaign for the new HQ. Local influential figures from the world of business, the arts, education and media attended the event, which focused on the final fundraising campaign to complete the building.

The new building will be a significant statement in the public realm proclaiming NBT's presence in Leeds city centre and providing a significant contribution to the dance and arts community in general.

Building work is due to start in Spring 2003 with the estimated completion date set for the end of 2004.

***Far left:*** *A scene from the acclaimed production of* Wuthering Heights. *Photo: Brian Slater.* ***Left:*** *The artist's impression of the proposed new headquarters for NBT and Phoenix Dance Theatre.*

# Variety is the spice of life

'**M**y Lords, Ladeeees and Gentlemen!' Who can ever forget Leonard Sachs and his inimitable performance as the chairman of television's The Good Old Days?

The City Varieties Music Hall grew out of a singing room built by landlord Charles Thornton in 1865 as an annex to the old White Swan coaching inn.

'Thornton's New Music Hall and Fashionable Lounge' changed its name to The City Varieties Music Hall in 1894, three years later it had on its boards 'Eight Lancashire Lads', a group of clog dancers featuring one Charles Chaplin who would later find immortal fame as a star of the silent screen.

Over the following decades music hall would go into gradual decline and ownership changed several times. In 1953 however the music hall was used for a pilot programme of a new series, The Good Old Days, produced and directed by Barney Colehan for BBC Television. In 1954 the Headrow door became the main entrance instead of the one on Swan Street. By 1960 The City Varieties was 'scheduled' as a building of special architectural and historical interest. In 1991 a new box office opened with the refurbishment of the original Victorian entrance on the newly restored Swan Street.

The final programme of BBC TV's The Good Old days was broadcast in 1983. The premises were sold to the Leeds Grand Theatre & Opera House Ltd in 1987 and the following year saw the re-launch of the Good Old Days as a stage show, under the continued direction of Barney Colehan until his death in 1991.

But the history of the City Varieties in the 20th century is not just about The Good Old Days; it is also home to great comedy, children's shows and music of all descriptions. Pantomime was restored as a regular annual feature at the music hall in 1968 after an absence of 20 years, whilst other performers include two ghosts. Today the City Varieties is also home to the City Varieties Youth Theatre and a Summer Youth Project, an annual opportunity for talented youngsters to learn about performing in, and managing, a theatre. Further along the spectrum are 'Silver Stars' - Britain's biggest amateur talent competition for the over 60s as well as the Potato Room Players, the City Varieties' very own amateur theatre company. There's nothing like variety!

*Top left:* A Theatre publicity poster from 1900.
*Below:* This photograph, dating from circa 1900 shows that the City Varieties has always been as popular as it is today. *Bottom:* One of a great number of appearances in the 'Good Old Days' by Danny La Rue.

# A grand drama

**W**ho said that television would close all the cinemas, or that the movies would destroy the theatre? The truth is that nothing on the goggle box or the silver screen can ever replace the indescribable magic of a live performance. And Leeds folk are more fortunate than the citizens of many other cities in having a theatre superb enough to make every live performance one to savour.

Leeds Grand Theatre and Opera House has captivated audiences for more than a century with a wealth of entertainment ranging from ballet to review, and through comedy and drama to musicals and pantomime.

Since its opening on 18th November 1878, all of the great names of theatre have trodden the boards at the Grand: Ellen Terry, Lily Langtry, Sarah Berhardt, Lord Olivier , Dame Sybil Thorndike and Ivor Novello.

In more recent decades the theatre has witnessed performances by Deborah Kerr, Ken Dodd, Tommy Steele, David Essex, Hank Marvin, Ben Elton and a galaxy of other stars. Built by architect George Corson, the theatre is a mixture of styles with a Gothic facade that belies the interior splendour. With a seating capacity of 1,550, The Grand is the largest theatre in Leeds: it has a classic proscenium arch with stalls, dress circle, balconies and boxes.

The Grand Theatre has become synonymous with all that is best in the performing arts. For more than a quarter of a century the theatre has been home to Opera North, one of Britain's best-loved and most highly respected opera companies. The theatre frequently stages hit West End and Broadway musicals and continues to attract the biggest names in show business to perform on its stage.

Over the years the Grand has established and maintained close links with some of the most prestigious touring companies, including Northern Ballet Theatre and English National Ballet in addition to local amateur operatic  and drama societies.

Today Leeds Grand Theatre and Opera House is recognised as a centre of excellence for entertainment and culture not only in the North of England but it is also one of the most popular theatres in the country.

**Top left:** *A 19th century view of Leeds Grand Theatre.*
**Left and below:** *The impressive Auditorium and stage of Leeds Grand Theatre and Opera House.*

# *Raising the roof!*

The West Yorkshire Playhouse began life in 1964 when a voluntary committee was set up of people who were passionate about and committed to starting up a professional producing theatre to serve West Yorkshire.

After tireless campaigning and fundraising, they opened up as the Leeds Playhouse in 1970, using a converted Sports Hall on the Leeds University campus. In 1973 the theatre attracted its first public funding from the Metropolitan County of West Yorkshire. This began a longstanding funding partnership between the local authorities and the Arts Council of England.

In 1986, several funding bodies combined to make possible the construction of a purpose built theatre, between them raising in the region of 13 million pounds. They acquired space on the Quarry Hill redevelopment site in Leeds, then home to the Quarry Hill flats.

Once it was decided that the flats should be pulled down it took two years to completely demolish them. After they were demolished, a quarry was dug which the building now stands on. The quarry itself can house 1,000 people!

Now 12 years old, the West Yorkshire Playhouse is one of the largest purpose-built theatres in the UK. Its modernity gives it great advantages over other regional theatres, as its catering and conference facilities bring other income streams into the business. It was also designed to be as accessible as possible to people with physical disabilities so that all members of the community feel welcome. This accessibility extends into the company's working policy.

As a regional producing theatre, the West Yorkshire Playhouse aims not only to give cultural experiences to both the people of Leeds and West Yorkshire but also to gain an international reputation for its work.

The Playhouse usually produces up to 14 pieces of work each year for its two stages, its 350 seat Courtyard Theatre and the 750 seat Quarry Theatre. The work also includes a strong educational strand both within and outside of the venue. In addition to this the Playhouse also hosts the work of touring companies.

A landmark year for the Playhouse was 2002 when Jude Kelly left as Artistic Director. As a driving force of the remarkable committee behind the conception and building of the new Playhouse, her creativity, drive and energy translated those concepts into action placing the Playhouse at the forefront of theatre.

The West Yorkshire Playhouse is looking forward with great optimism to an equally creative and exciting artistic future under the leadership of Ian Brown, the newly appointed Artistic Director & Chief Executive, whose appointment will help to reinforce the Playhouse's position as the pre-eminent regional theatre in the country.

**Left and below:** *Two aspects of the West Yorkshire Playhouse at Quarry Hill.*

# A jewel in Yorkshire's crown

The British love affair with India has lasted for more than two hundred years; and measured by our continuing enjoyment of Indian food that love affair shows no signs of ending. The British East India Company began trading on the Indian sub-continent in the 18th century and acquired ever increasing influence there until the middle of the 19th century when the British government took over the company's responsibilities.

Unarguably the high point of the British presence in that vast and beautiful country would be Queen Victoria's assumption of the title Empress of India in 1876.

Though independence would be given to India and Pakistan in 1948, a process overseen by the British government's last Viceroy, Lord Mountbatten of Burma, by then the British had acquired a taste for the country - quite literally.

The first Indian restaurants had opened in London in the 19th century catering for the tastes of returning colonial officials; today that once rare cuisine is commonplace throughout the United Kingdom - most noticeably in Yorkshire which prides itself on prize-winning restaurants.

The Last Viceroy restaurant in Horsforth opened in 1985 as 'Indian Nights'.

Indian Nights did not do too well and Ishy, one of its present owners and who was then running a chain of Indian restaurants in North Yorkshire, was asked to help turn it around. He took over the restaurant in 1992 in partnership with his brothers Moh and Maj and changed the name to The Last Viceroy, a name which simultaneously not only referred to Lord Mountbatten, but also got away from the by then much overused restaurant names such as 'Pearl of India' and 'Taj Mahal'.

Not only was the restaurant now successful but another branch was soon to be opened in Shipley.

The delicious Kashmiri cuisine and stylish surroundings have resulted in numerous awards. The Last Viceroy was voted one of the top 200 restaurants in the country. Celebrities who have patronised the restaurant include Archbishop Tutu of South Africa, the Australian Cricket team, Jack Charlton, Steve Davis and the cast members of ITV's Emmerdale.

Meanwhile the love affair with India goes on and on.

***Below left:*** *Ishy, Moh and Maj outside their restaurant.*
***Below:*** *The welcoming main entrance to the restaurant.*

Residents of Park Street
celebrating VE Day.

# Acknowledgments

The publishers would like to thank

West Yorkshire Archive Service

Leeds City Libraries Local Studies Library

John Thornton

Kevin McIlroy

Steve Ainsworth

# True North Books Ltd - Book List

Memories of Accrington - 1 903204 05 4

Memories of Barnet - 1 903204 16 X

Memories of Barnsley - 1 900463 11 3

Golden Years of Barnsley -1 900463 87 3

Memories of Basingstoke - 1 903204 26 7

Memories of Bedford - 1 900463 83 0

More Memories of Bedford - 1 903204 33 X

Golden Years of Birmingham - 1 900463 04 0

Birmingham Memories - 1 903204 45 3

Memories of Blackburn - 1 900463 40 7

More Memories of Blackburn - 1 900463 96 2

Memories of Blackpool - 1 900463 21 0

Memories of Bolton - 1 900463 45 8

More Memories of Bolton - 1 900463 13 X

Bolton Memories - 1 903204 37 2

Memories of Bournemouth -1 900463 44 X

Memories of Bradford - 1 900463 00 8

More Memories of Bradford - 1 900463 16 4

More Memories of Bradford II - 1 900463 63 6

Bradford Memories - 1 903204 47 X

Bradford City Memories - 1 900463 57 1

Memories of Bristol - 1 900463 78 4

More Memories of Bristol - 1 903204 43 7

Memories of Bromley - 1 903204 21 6

Memories of Burnley - 1 900463 95 4

Golden Years of Burnley - 1 900463 67 9

Memories of Bury - 1 900463 90 3

Memories of Cambridge - 1 900463 88 1

Memories of Cardiff - 1 900463 14 8

Memories of Carlisle - 1 900463 38 5

Memories of Chelmsford - 1 903204 29 1

Memories of Cheltenham - 1 903204 17 8

Memories of Chester - 1 900463 46 6

More Memories of Chester -1 903204 02 X

Memories of Chesterfield -1 900463 61 X

More Memories of Chesterfield - 1 903204 28 3

Memories of Colchester - 1 900463 74 1

Nostalgic Coventry - 1 900463 58 X

Coventry Memories - 1 903204 38 0

Memories of Croydon - 1 900463 19 9

More Memories of Croydon - 1 903204 35 6

Golden Years of Darlington - 1 900463 72 5

Nostalgic Darlington - 1 900463 31 8

Darlington Memories - 1 903204 46 1

Memories of Derby - 1 900463 37 7

More Memories of Derby - 1 903204 20 8

Memories of Dewsbury & Batley - 1 900463 80 6

Memories of Doncaster - 1 900463 36 9

Nostalgic Dudley - 1 900463 03 2

Golden Years of Dudley - 1 903204 60 7

Memories of Edinburgh - 1 900463 33 4

Memories of Enfield - 1 903204 14 3

Memories of Exeter - 1 900463 94 6

Memories of Glasgow - 1 900463 68 7

More Memories of Glasgow - 1 903204 44 5

Memories of Gloucester - 1 903204 04 6

Memories of Grimsby - 1 900463 97 0

More Memories of Grimsby - 1 903204 36 4

Memories of Guildford - 1 903204 22 4

Memories of Halifax - 1 900463 05 9

More Memories of Halifax - 1 900463 06 7

Golden Years of Halifax - 1 900463 62 8

Nostalgic Halifax - 1 903204 30 5

Memories of Harrogate - 1 903204 01 1

Memories of Hartlepool - 1 900463 42 3

Memories of High Wycombe - 1 900463 84 9

Memories of Huddersfield - 1 900463 15 6

More Memories of Huddersfield - 1 900463 26 1

Golden Years of Huddersfield - 1 900463 77 6

Nostalgic Huddersfield - 1 903204 19 4

Huddersfield Town FC - 1 900463 51 2

Memories of Hull - 1 900463 86 5

More Memories of Hull - 1 903204 06 2

Memories of Ipswich - 1 900463 09 1

More Memories of Ipswich - 1 903204 52 6

Memories of Keighley - 1 900463 01 6

Golden Years of Keighley - 1 900463 92 X

Memories of Kingston - 1 903204 24 0

# True North Books Ltd - Book List

Memories of Leeds - 1 900463 75 X

More Memories of Leeds - 1 900463 12 1

Golden Years of Leeds - 1 903204 07 0

Memories of Leicester - 1 900463 08 3

More Memories of Leicester - 1 903204 08 9

Memories of Leigh - 1 903204 27 5

Memories of Lincoln - 1 900463 43 1

Memories of Liverpool - 1 900463 07 5

More Memories of Liverpool - 1 903204 09 7

Liverpool Memories - 1 903204 53 4

Memories of Luton - 1 900463 93 8

Memories of Macclesfield - 1 900463 28 8

Memories of Manchester - 1 900463 27 X

More Memories of Manchester - 1 903204 03 8

Manchester Memories - 1 903204 54 2

Memories of Middlesbrough - 1 900463 56 3

More Memories of Middlesbrough - 1 903204 42 9

Memories of Newbury - 1 900463 79 2

Memories of Newcastle - 1 900463 81 4

More Memories of Newcastle - 1 903204 10 0

Memories of Newport - 1 900463 59 8

Memories of Northampton - 1 900463 48 2

More Memories of Northampton - 1 903204 34 8

Memories of Norwich - 1 900463 73 3

Memories of Nottingham - 1 900463 91 1

More Memories of Nottingham - 1 903204 11 9

Bygone Oldham - 1 900463 25 3

Memories of Oldham - 1 900463 76 8

Memories of Oxford - 1 900463 54 7

Memories of Peterborough - 1 900463 98 9

Golden Years of Poole - 1 900463 69 5

Memories of Portsmouth - 1 900463 39 3

More Memories of Portsmouth - 1 903204 51 8

Nostalgic Preston - 1 900463 50 4

More Memories of Preston - 1 900463 17 2

Preston Memories - 1 903204 41 0

Memories of Reading - 1 900463 49 0

Memories of Rochdale - 1 900463 60 1

More Memories of Reading - 1 903204 39 9

More Memories of Rochdale - 1 900463 22 9

Memories of Romford - 1 903204 40 2

Memories of St Albans - 1 903204 23 2

Memories of St Helens - 1 900463 52 0

Memories of Sheffield - 1 900463 20 2

More Memories of Sheffield - 1 900463 32 6

Golden Years of Sheffield - 1 903204 13 5

Memories of Slough - 1 900 463 29 6

Golden Years of Solihull - 1 903204 55 0

Memories of Southampton - 1 900463 34 2

More Memories of Southampton - 1 903204 49 6

Memories of Stockport - 1 900463 55 5

More Memories of Stockport - 1 903204 18 6

Memories of Stockton - 1 900463 41 5

Memories of Stoke-on-Trent - 1 900463 47 4

More Memories of Stoke-on-Trent - 1 903204 12 7

Memories of Stourbridge - 1903204 31 3

Memories of Sunderland - 1 900463 71 7

More Memories of Sunderland - 1 903204 48 8

Memories of Swindon - 1 903204 00 3

Memories of Uxbridge - 1 900463 64 4

Memories of Wakefield - 1 900463 65 2

More Memories of Wakefield - 1 900463 89 X

Nostalgic Walsall - 1 900463 18 0

Golden Years of Walsall - 1 903204 56 9

More Memories of Warrington - 1 900463 02 4

Memories of Watford - 1 900463 24 5

Golden Years of West Bromwich - 1 900463 99 7

Memories of Wigan  - 1 900463 85 7

Golden Years of Wigan - 1 900463 82 2

Nostalgic Wirral - 1 903204 15 1

Memories of Woking - 1 903204 32 1

Nostalgic Wolverhampton - 1 900463 53 9

Wolverhampton Memories - 1 903204 50 X

Memories of Worcester - 1 903204 25 9

Memories of Wrexham - 1 900463 23 7

Memories of York - 1 900463 66 0